PROVOKING SUDDEN PROPHETIC INTERVENTION

Unusual Rise and Elevation

David S. Philemon

Royal Diadem Publishing Inc.

Dedication

To the Almighty God, my foundation and ever-present help. I am grateful for Your boundless love and grace that sustain me daily. And to my mentor in ministry, Rev. George Izunwa, whose steadfast commitment to the call of God has deeply impacted my life. Your guidance and support have been invaluable, encouraging me to walk boldly in the path God has set before me. Thank you for your example and your heart for the Kingdom.

ACKNOWLEDGMENTS

This book would not have been possible without the unwavering support, dedication, and talent of an extraordinary team. My deepest gratitude goes to each of you for your contributions, insights, and encouragement throughout this journey.

First and foremost, thank you to Rev. Mimi Philemon my dear wife, Rev. Shina Gentry, and and my assistant pastor Rev. Bright Amudoaghan for your incredible effort, encouragement, and belief in this project. Your support has been instrumental in bringing this vision to life.

To the dedicated leaders of Royal Diadem Publishing, Ide Imogie and Kishawna Bailey, I am immensely grateful for your belief in this project from the very beginning and for investing your time and energy into its development. Your creativity, dedication, and expertise have been the backbone of this endeavor.

I am especially grateful to the Royal Diadem Publishing team— Beulah Orogun, Emmanuella Ben-Eboh, Doyinsade Awodele, Kim Matthews, and Shante Gill, for your meticulous attention to detail, refining every page and ensuring that each word reflects our vision.

A heartfelt thank you to my family, friends, and colleagues whose unwavering support and belief in this project gave me the courage and strength to see it through.

Finally, thank you to all the readers and supporters who make this work meaningful. I am humbled and honored to share this journey with each of you.

With all my gratitude,
David Philemon

CONTENTS

INTRODUCTION

I n a constantly changing and evolving world, 2024 is a critical year for you personally and humanity. This year, especially its second quarter, is significant for your life, relevance, and the long-term effects of your existence. New possibilities present themselves every day and every month. These are times to look ahead, let go of things that no longer serve you, and get in a position to enter God's divine plan. Chaos can quickly sneak into your life and obstruct your development if you don't control what comes and goes out of it. But you are more significant than you might know, and your actions count, not just to you but also to God and your generation. You are not here by accident but by design, and there is always a chance for divine intervention.

During this time of year, it is crucial to recognize that one prudent action, one perceptive choice, may act as a spark to connect your life with God's plan. You'll understand that today is more than another day on the calendar as we go deeper into this book. Like Zerubbabel, who understood the significance of his role in carrying out God's plan, you have a divine opportunity to mold your destiny (Zechariah 4:6). The lesson is obvious: you cannot genuinely flourish in life until you recognize how necessary your actions are to God's grand scheme. Satan tries to distract you from this awareness and make you tired, but you must fight him. Your life, decisions, and actions are essential for advancing God's kingdom on earth and for you.

As we embark on this path, remember the importance of choices: what you accept and project into your life has a significant impact. Your decisions will determine how your life turns out, whether you decide to give your acts meaning or eliminate problems that stand in the way of your advancement. God has laid the foundation for your significant, essential, rather than insignificant efforts.

This book is a manual for anyone looking for supernatural help in a world where hardship is taking on a more dominant role. It provides a path to breaking through obstacles and fulfilling one's destiny. With God's anointing, you may accomplish goals in months or even days that would take others decades. When one accepts divine impartation, the seemingly impossible becomes achievable. Walking by God's grace condenses years of development into a single instant, enabling remarkable accomplishments.

This journey is about more than just planning and goal-setting; it's about receiving an impartation from God that will propel you to heights of achievement and elevation beyond your capacity to reach. Your biggest obstacles can become roadblocks on the way to triumph if you apply this impartation, which you will learn more about in the following chapters. When you fully embrace the anointing that God is prepared to pour forth over your life, mountains will become molehills, and giants will become bread.

After reading this book, you will desire a more intimate, personal relationship with God. Living a life that honors God in every manner is more important than pursuing material wealth or success. It's also about establishing oneself as a wise, respected, and well-respected person. Scriptures such as Proverbs 8:12–21 (MSG) include wisdom, indicating that when one aligns oneself with God's plan, one can reach realms of plenty, favor, and success beyond human comprehension.

As you read this book, you will learn how to deliver this impartation through faith, prayer, and prophetic announcements.

Each chapter has scripture references, prayers, and prophetic utterances to help you embrace a life of great victories and overcome setbacks with consistent victories by the power of the anointing. You can dwell in God's unending favor and access supernatural understanding and spiritual clarity.

Many people suffer from sentiments of directionlessness and insignificance in today's fast-paced society.

This book emphasizes that each person has a special place in God's larger plan, which means that for anyone to overcome those challenges, they must acknowledge their place. God has a purpose for our existence; it is not random.

The first chapter, "Recognize the Importance of Your Existence," establishes the groundwork for this trip by exploring the profound reality that God uniquely creates every individual and has a purpose. Acknowledging this reality will enable everyone to bring meaning into all facets of life and synchronize their aspirations with God's divine design.

You will learn about the importance of spiritual alignment as you go through the chapters, as this is a recurrent theme in the book. Putting your will in line with God's will allows blessings to come your way, enhancing your life and enabling you to help others. As you also read this book "Becoming a Distribution Center of God's Blessings," you will learn how to act as a conduit for God's blessings so that less fortunate people can take advantage of the abundance of His favor around you.

This journey will also test your ability to move beyond accepting life's "appetizers" to engaging in its "main course." Many individuals grow comfortable with shallow experiences, missing the depth and richness God intended for them. You have to embrace obedience and sacrifice if you want to fulfill your spiritual mission. This chapter, "The Power of Sacrifice and Obedience," will discuss how these qualities lead to increased accountability and spiritual development.

Another crucial aspect of this trip is timing. When you align yourself with God's timeline, you can have more peace and confidence in overcoming life's difficulties. "Instructions for Unusual Lifting provides practical methods for improving every aspect of your life. This will grant you the privilege of realizing the potential that has lain dormant in you for far too long.

This book eventually ends with a set of prophetic statements and prayers meant to give you strength. In "The Prophetic Process in Discovering Destiny," you will discover how God's unique plan for your life can be revealed through prophecy and prayer. This book is a useful manual for spiritual development rather than merely a conceptual investigation.

As you peruse these chapters, get ready to be blessed. God is making a unique arrangement for you to provide an incredible mental and emotional experience. I pray that your reading will attract a season of extraordinary breakthroughs, divine elevation, and recognition of your place in God's larger plan in the mighty name of JESUS. (Amen)

CHAPTER 1

RECOGNIZING THE SIGNIFICANCE OF YOUR EXISTENCE

L ife's grumpy road can frequently seem daunting, full of unknowns, detours, and times when we wonder if our own lives matter in the big picture. The reality is that every life matters; yours, in particular, has a divine purpose entirely tied to God's eternal plan. The difficulty is seeing how important this is and aligning your choices, behaviors, and viewpoints with what God has precisely planned for you.

You Are Not a Coincidence!

God has a unique plan for you from the time of your conception. If you are still here today, you obviously have a part to play in furthering God's kingdom on earth. You exist not by happenstance or accident. Your personality, your gifts, your circumstances—in fact, everything about you—has been divinely designed to fulfill a mission that only you can achieve.

Zechariah 4:6 tells the story of Zerubbabel, a leader called to rebuild Jerusalem's temple. God reminded him in the middle of his challenging endeavor that it would be God's Spirit, not human might or might, that would bring him success. You are currently subject to the same truth. You may feel that the obstacles in your life are overwhelming or that you are insufficient for the task before you, but God is saying that your significance resides not in what you can do by yourself but in what He can do through you.

You, too, must awaken to the realization that your existence has a divine assignment, just as Zerubbabel had to grasp the gravity and significance of his mission. This goes beyond only becoming successful personally or becoming well-known in the outside world. It's about aligning your schedule with that of heaven and turning it into a tool to carry out God's purposes.

Fighting for Significance

The struggle against insignificance is among the most critical conflicts we encounter in life. Satan, the enemy of your soul, is always trying to make you feel less important by telling you things like you are unimportant, that your efforts are in vain, or that someone else might easily take your place. Satan is skilled at making you feel worn out, exhausted, and unproductive. If you give in to these emotions, you may give up on your mission.

The fact is, though, that small thing you are doing matters. Your life's labor is an essential component of God's more extensive design, even if it appears minor or ignored by others. Similar to how Zerubbabel's quest to build a temple seemed to be a physical undertaking, it was a spiritual purpose that would impact future generations. Even if the work you are called to do may not always seem exciting, it has the power to change the lives of as many watching in very unexpected ways.

Think about how history remembers those who embraced their heavenly responsibilities. Hmmm! Because Zerubbabel believed that the challenge before him was significant, his name appears in the Bible today. Discussing Zerubbabel's leadership and loyalty thousands of years later is still relevant.

Failure to follow the path God has set for you will impact future generations and your life. In many years to come, people will talk about your performance, or they will talk about a lack of it in completing your assignment.

The Influence of Following God's Plan

Knowing that your life matters is not enough; you must also realize how important it is to align with God's plan. Your life is part of God's divine plan for the earth. He wants you to walk in harmony with the Holy Spirit and by His will. True success rests in this alignment since God's strength flows through people who agree with His purpose.

How do you fit into God's plan? Intentionality is where it all starts. Seeking God's plan for your life requires intentionality, and you need to be receptive to the Holy Spirit's guidance. One method to get started is projecting the things that God wants you to accomplish and ejecting anything that gets in the way of His plans.

We frequently undervalue the ability to project and eject. God desires you to "project" certain things—such as faith, purpose, and an excellence-driven mindset—across your days, months, and years. Contradictions like diversions worry, and doubt are also things you must "eject" from your life. You will allow darkness and confusion to control your destiny if you do not take responsibility for the images you bring into each stage of your life. You must choose carefully what to let in and keep out.

The Bible makes it very evident how vital this alignment is. **"Your favor made me as secure as a mountain," according to Psalm 30:7 TLB.** Following God's plan, you become as trustworthy, stable, and safe as a mountain. The enemy will always attempt to offer you pebbles rather than mountains, meaning he will make minor, unimportant attempts to divert your attention from God's larger purpose. Never accept anything less than the highest peaks God has in store for you.

The Value of Being Aware of Your Position in the Kingdom

Your contribution to God's Kingdom is directly related to the significance of your existence. Every accomplishment made by one of God's children contributes to the growth of His Kingdom on earth. This is about Kingdom success, not simply personal accomplishments, the type of success that advances God's objectives and positively impacts the lives of others.

How well you fit into the greater scheme of what God is accomplishing in the world is how you will be judged for the significance of your life. You will lose out on the divine plan that is supposed to unfold in your life if you reject your calling or live simply for yourself. **Every child of God has significance in the Kingdom, and each little victory adds to the grand success of God's plans for the world.**

The devil knows this, so he makes a solid effort to make you feel unimportant. He is aware that living by God jeopardizes his dominion of darkness. As soon as you start living out your calling, you contribute to expanding, advancing, and restoring God's Kingdom. On the other hand, the enemy's schemes are advanced, and the growth of God's Kingdom is impeded when you back down or refuse to accept your purpose.

God Unites Everything Through One Item

Knowing that God can use one thing you do well to make everything else fall into place is another essential component of realizing your significance. Sometimes, all it takes to start experiencing a string of miraculous breakthroughs in your life is one obedience step, epiphany, or wise choice.

God frequently gives people a prophetic shift during services or meetings; this is the point at which things begin to make sense. Have faith that God can use the one thing you're doing well to catalyze change in every other aspect of your life, even if you've been stuck or unclear about your direction.

For this reason, today is significant. Every day, you have the chance to have profound experiences with God that have the power to alter your life. What looks unimportant now might hold the key to opening up important doors later on. When he recognized his importance, everything changed for Zerubbabel, his people, and future generations.

A Prompt to Lead a Purposeful Life

You do have an option, however. You have two options: either you accept a life of insignificance and lose out on the amazing things God has in store for you, or you choose to live a life that aligns with God's agenda and experience the fullness of His purpose. Your life is still being written, and your decisions today will decide how that story unfolds.

Living purposefully involves pushing past distractions and lies and persuading you that your life isn't necessary. It entails accepting the reality that you were made for a purpose, and that purpose is essential. It also entails realizing how vital God's time is. Not every day is a component of God's schedule for massive transformations, but every day is an opportunity to prepare yourself for those miraculous moments when everything changes.

Remember this as you embrace your purpose to the fullest: your life matters. You matter to God, your age, and God's Kingdom. You are expected to make an impression and shine brightly for the good of God's long-term plan and your advantage. Acknowledge the importance of your life and let God use it to illuminate the way for others, to give them hope and meaning.

CHAPTER 2

PROJECTING INTO PURPOSE

L ife is a series of seasons, each filled with opportunities and challenges that shape our journey toward fulfilling God's divine purpose. As believers, we are called to live intentionally, understanding that every day, month, and year presents a chance to project God's light into our path. This means actively engaging with the present while watching the future, ensuring our steps align with God's will. Simultaneously, we must eject anything that contradicts His purpose for our lives.

Understanding Spiritual Projection

Spiritual projection means taking the initiative to shape your life to fit God's plan. It's easy to live life inertly, reacting to things as they happen. But to project into purpose, you must consciously create an atmosphere conducive to achievement, spiritual growth, and divine favor through your behaviors and attitudes.

Psalm 30:7 TLB declares, "Your favor made me as secure as a mountain," an essential verse to examine. This verse emphasizes the stability and security that come from God's favor. Just as mountains are firm, steadfast, and eternal, so too may our lives be when they are firmly anchored in God's design. When we look ahead, we are pleading with God to guide us, to make our foundation solid and our paths straight.

Using this projection, you can take charge of the spiritual environment around you, similar to how an architect plans a building's layout. A building's structure wouldn't be left up to chance in the hopes that it would be sturdy and attractive. Similarly, you can't let fate decide your life's mission. Instead, you create the conditions necessary for God's purpose to pass via prayer, declarations, and deliberate deeds.

The Importance of Daily Intentionality: Living on Purpose

Every day offers fresh opportunities to live with intention. God sees every day as necessary, even if we occasionally consider life a series of routine days. You must incorporate a sense of purpose into your everyday activities because you realize that modest yet dependable deeds provide the groundwork for bigger things. It's simple to believe that a select few significant life events determine our fate, yet more often than not, our daily choices determine our identity and direction.

The Bible explains today's power: **"This is the day the Lord has made; let us rejoice and be glad in it," declares Psalm 118:24.** God has given us each day as a gift, and we have an obligation to make the most of it. Your actions today can shape your future, and your projections into today have a lasting impact on your life.

How do you start every day with intention? A potent method involves using biblical declarations and prayer. Every morning, when you wake up, speak the promises of God over your life. Speak the Word of God into your situation and believe His favor will envelop you like a shield. Start your day by visualizing the security of being as secure as a mountain, just as Psalm 30:7 describes. You invite God's presence to lead and guard you through life's possibilities and problems when you announce His favor over your life daily.

Ejecting Contradictions: Removing What Does Not Belong

Projecting God's purpose into your life is crucial, but so is removing things that don't belong. Contradictions and evil forces attempt to enter our lives and draw us away from God's intended path for us. Contradictions can take many different forms, such as unfavorable ideas, immoral behaviors, poisonous relationships, or anything else that goes against what God has revealed.

The spiritual battle is what it takes to drive out these forces. According to the Bible, we are fighting spiritual powers of evil rather than physical forces of flesh and blood (Ephesians 6:12). This calls on us to look for anything that can compromise our relationship with God and guard our hearts and thoughts accordingly. We need to act to eject negative influences before they cause spiritual harm, just as a pilot would leave a malfunctioning aircraft to avoid tragedy.

To eject effectively, you must identify the contradictions in your life. This calls for discernment. Contradictions can be overt in some situations, like sinful behavior or toxic relationships, or covert in others, like procrastination, fear, or doubt. These subtle contradictions may undermine your ability to project purpose into your life. They might begin as little diversion, but they have the potential to cause severe delays in achieving your divinely appointed goals.

The enemy frequently uses distraction and discouragement as a tactic. For example, he may use fear to keep you from acting in faith, doubt to make you wonder if God's promises are for you or busyness to keep your attention on unimportant things. It is essential to cast out these contradictions as soon as you see them.

God's Light Projected in Every Season

Every stage of life has its chances and problems. While certain seasons are joyful and abundant, others may feel hard and arid. It's critical to bring God's light into every season. God's light symbolizes His direction, truth, and presence. When you get His light into every season, you allow God to guide and light your way.

Consider the waiting season in this way.

A common reason why people suffer during waiting seasons is a sense of not moving closer to their mission. But God is still at work when we wait. You can use your time while you wait to strengthen your relationship with God, learn new talents, or advance spiritually by projecting His light into it. Waiting is an opportunity to prepare for the next season of purpose, not a sign of passivity.

It's crucial to reflect God's light throughout prosperous times. Sometimes, success might cause us to lose sight of our reliance on God. Instead of asking God for direction, we might rely more on our abilities or knowledge. However, when we project God's light into our prosperity, we stay humble, realizing that all good things come from Him. His light ensures that our success is consistent with His desire rather than diverting us from His purpose.

God's light can change any season—whether it is marked by adversity, waiting, or success—and illuminate your path. It provides guidance, clarity, and the bravery to continue forward motion.

Rejecting Darkness

God's light must be projected upon us, but we must also work hard to push back the darkness. Darkness signifies confusion, deception, and anything that undermines God's truth. It may show up as spiritual blindness, dread, anxiety, or temptation. The enemy uses darkness to impair our judgment and divert us from our goal.

The Bible is one of the main tools we have to fight darkness. Psalm 119:105 says that the Bible is a light for our path and a candle for our feet. Scripture meditation clears the confusion and lies of the enemy from our minds by supplying God's truth. If you want to fight darkness in your life, spend as much time as possible in the Word. Let it guide your decisions, ideas, and actions.

Another way to reject darkness is through community. God meant for us to coexist harmoniously as believers. Being a part of a strong Christian fellowship helps us better resist the enemy's tactics. We receive support, accountability, and encouragement from fellow Christians, who also assist us in maintaining our focus on God's plan. Conversely, the enemy employs isolation to draw us into the dark side. Stay connected to a community that reflects God's light.

Finding Meaning in Everything

Acknowledging the significance of each moment is among the most exquisite features of projecting into purpose. God is concerned with the significant decisions that alter our lives and the minor ones we make daily. Imbue your life with meaning, and open yourself up to divine guidance and favor in all aspects.

Nothing in your life is too small for God to be concerned about. Whatever decisions you make in life—about your relationships, work, or daily schedule—impact achieving your mission.

Believe that God is at work even when nothing important is happening. **Breakthroughs in the great things are frequently the result of faithfulness in the minor things.** Never undervalue the influence of routine obedience. God often sets us up for great purposes during mundane times.

CHAPTER 3

THE POWER OF
SPIRITUAL ALIGNMENT

Our choices and actions on a physical level influence life, as do the spiritual forces we choose to follow. Let us see the vital significance of spiritual alignment: aligning oneself with the forces that facilitate success and staying away from the spirits that bring about failure. Gaining insight into the spiritual aspect of accomplishments and setbacks can change our lives and guide us toward realizing God's plan for us.

The Necessity of Spiritual Alignment: What Does It Mean?

The process of aligning your life with God's will and divine goal is known as spiritual alignment. Our lives must be spiritually connected for us to proceed successfully, just as a car has to be to drive straight and true. When we align with God's plan, we put ourselves in a position to receive God's strength, favor, and guidance.

Spiritual sensitivity, or the capacity to perceive God's hand in your life and hear His voice, is essential to this spiritual connection. Many people lead lives divorced from God's plan, just like Gideon did in Judges 6:13 TLB when he fled his calling. Threshing wheat at a winepress was Gideon's job until God called him to something more significant: defending Israel from their attackers. Gideon's account reveals that we can be misaligned with our higher purpose even when we do it in a way that feels essential or proper.

Spiritual alignment entails being open to divine disruptions or when God intervenes in your daily life to inspire you to pursue higher goals. When you have spiritual sensitivity, you can discern God's will for your life and answer His call, even when it conflicts with your plans.

The Spirit of Failure vs. The Spirit of Achievement

The fundamental component of spiritual alignment is understanding that spiritual influences impact success and failure. **Spiritual success is about realizing the purpose for which God created you, not for achieving personal goals or worldly prosperity.** However, failure occurs when our will is not in line with God's, whether due to sin, distraction, or a refusal to follow His guidance.

Alignment with God's power, grace, and direction is a hallmark of the victorious spirit. It results from living by God's plan and using His strength rather than just one's might. **"Unless the Lord builds the house, the builders labor in vain," states Psalm 127:1.** This verse emphasizes the pointlessness of attempting to succeed independently without God's help. Success is not just conceivable but certain when we align ourselves with His intentions since we collaborate with the supernatural.

On the other hand, when we attempt to achieve success outside of God's will, we give rise to the spirit of failure. Because it stems from human striving rather than heavenly empowerment, this spirit is typically accompanied by perplexity, frustration, and tiredness. Gideon's early actions were motivated by a spirit of failure; he was terrified, ran away from his adversaries, and was blind to the potential that God saw in him. But after he put his will in line with God's, Gideon went from being a failure to a success, helping Israel defeat their oppressors.

Even if something looks promising at first, not all possibilities or roads lead to success, and understanding this is essential to avoiding the spirit of failure. Without spiritual connection, we could embark on endeavors that prove to be fruitless since God never intended them.

Before making decisions that will affect your future, whether they relate to your relationships, work, or personal objectives, it is imperative that you contact God. When we seek His direction, we link ourselves with the spirit of success.

How Your Path Is Affected by Your Spiritual Sensitivity to God's Agenda

Spiritual alignment is one of its most potent effects. Your current alignment with spiritual energies determines your destiny in life. Even though the journey may appear challenging at times, you are headed toward spiritual success if you are attuned to God's agenda and proceed by His will.

Obedience and discernment are both necessary for spiritual sensitivity. The capacity to discern the spiritual reality concealed beneath what the natural world presents is discernment. For instance, Gideon's priorities were the direct problems he faced—the Midianites' mistreatment of Israel—but he lacked perspective in the broader picture. Gideon was blind to the extent of God's calling, even though God had already predestined him to be a deliverer for his people.

God frequently communicates to us subtly, and when we're preoccupied with the things of life, it's simple to ignore His message. For this reason, it is crucial to maintain a close relationship with God through prayer, meditation, and reading His Word to be spiritually aligned. Spending time in His presence will make you more sensitive to His guidance and discern when He is pointing you in a specific direction.

The second essential component of spiritual sensitivity is obedience. The following action you take after discerning God's will is obedience, even if it means moving outside your comfort zone. Gideon needed to leave the protection of his hiding location and assume his leadership and warrior duties. Sacrifice is often required for obedience; it could involve giving up personal goals, time, or finances to follow God's plan. However, the advantage of compliance is that it sets you up for long-term success and happiness.

Dangers of Misalignment: How Failure Can Undermine Goals

Spiritual misalignment can result in disappointment, frustration, and lost opportunities, just as spiritual alignment can help you succeed. Misalignment arises when we ignore God's voice or choose our path over His desire. The Bible is replete with instances of people who failed and faced setbacks because their goals did not align with God's.

Consider Saul's history as Israel's first king. While Saul had God's favor at the start of his reign, his disobedience eventually caused him to become spiritually unbalanced. Saul decided to take matters into his own hands and acted out of fear rather than faith instead of waiting for the prophet Samuel to make offerings. His downfall resulted from his disobedience, and David, a man who identified with God's heart, replaced him in the end (1 Samuel 13:14).

A lesson from Saul's story is that chances and heavenly favor can be lost due to misalignment. Our activities can backfire if they do not align with God's plan, even when we believe we are doing what is best for us or others. A tendency to take charge of our destiny and a lack of faith in God's timing are two common causes of misalignment.

Remaining Fixed on God's Will to Prevent Spiritual Drift

One of the challenges of staying in spiritual alignment is avoiding spiritual drift. Spiritual drift occurs when we progressively stray from God's plan, often without realizing it. It can happen when we get overly fixated on our goals, be they personal, material, or worldly accomplishments. With time, we can discover that we have strayed from God's path and wonder why we feel stuck or unfulfilled.

It's crucial to continually assess your alignment with God's will to prevent spiritual wandering. This means you allow humility and the readiness to change directions when needed. It's simple to slip off course when we seek God's wisdom rather than relying on our understanding.

We can also experience spiritual drift when we grow comfortable with our beliefs. If we cease seeking His presence and listening for His voice, we risk making judgments based more on our wants than God's purpose. We must actively seek His presence to be firmly rooted in God's plan. To prevent being swept away by the tides of the world, we must stay firmly anchored to God's Word, prayer, and the direction of the Holy Spirit, much like a ship in a harbor.

Leading a Spiritually Aligned Life: Doable Actions

To make the correct spiritual alignments, dedication, and awareness are required. The following valuable actions can assist you in maintaining your spiritual alignment with God's plan:

- Daily Surrender: At the start of each day, give God your plans, goals, and decisions. Seek His guidance and align your heart with His will.

- Seek God's Direction: Spend some time in prayer and seeking God's direction before making important decisions. Don't act hastily without first speaking with Him.

- Be Open to Divine Interruptions: Just like Gideon, keep your eyes open for the chance that God might summon you to something out of the ordinary. When He breaks up your schedule, be prepared to pay attention and comply.

- Surround Yourself with Godly Counsel: Ask wise, experienced Christians for guidance on discerning God's will. God occasionally uses other people to affirm His plan for your life.

- **Stay Rooted in God's Word**: The Bible is your roadmap for spiritual alignment. Make it a priority to read and meditate on Scripture daily, allowing it to shape your decisions and actions.

CHAPTER 4

BECOMING A DISTRIBUTION CENTER OF GOD'S BLESSINGS

God's blessings are intended to flow through us and impact others, not end with us. This chapter will look at the idea of being a hub for God's blessings. This means realizing that God wants to use you to spread His goodness to everyone around you and you. You open yourself up to more riches in all aspects of your life when you put yourself in a position to accept and give blessings. Distractions can, however, also be dangerous since they might prevent you from seeing heavenly appointments and chances to bless others.

God's Intention for You to Serve as a Warehouse

When we consider blessings, we usually concentrate on what we want or need from God. But God's blessings are intended to do more for us than just satisfy our material wants; they are designed to enable us to benefit others. **This sense of abundance and invitation is summed up in Luke 14:17–18 TPT: "When the banquet was ready, he sent his servant to tell the guests, 'Come, for everything is now ready.'"** But one by one, they all started offering justifications.

In this story, God asks His people to join in His rich blessings, symbolized by the banquet. The issue is that many individuals are preoccupied with their problems and fail to notice the invitation. This is a potent reminder that although God wants to show us His kindness, it is not only for our benefit. God desires us to serve as conduits, or distribution points, via which His gifts are extended to others. We risk missing this bigger goal if we are preoccupied with ourselves or drawn to unimportant things.

Getting More Than You Can Give Away

Receiving more than you require to become a distributor center entails sharing with others rather than hoarding for your gain. A distribution center is where items are received, processed, and shipped to different places in the real world. In a spiritual sense, God wants to shower you with blessings so you might share them with others rather than merely hoarding them for yourself.

The Bible is replete with instances of people who were richly blessed by God, enabling them to bless others. Consider Abraham, to whom God said in Genesis 12:2 NKJV , "I will bless you and make your name great, and you shall be a blessing," and he would create a vast nation. Abraham bestowed benefits upon all the nations of the world, not only his own family. God also want to bless you in ways that touch other people's lives in addition to your own.

When we embrace this principle, it affects the way we pray for and receive benefits. Knowing that we are called to be conduits of His generosity, we might petition God to increase our ability to accept more rather than merely asking for what we need to survive. With this mental change, we can go from a posture of scarcity—where we are always preoccupied with meeting our own needs—to a posture of plenty, where we actively seek out chances to give to and assist others.

The Generosity Heart: A Mirror of God's Essence

Being a distribution center is fundamentally about having a generous spirit, which reflects God's character. God is a provider. To save the world, He offered His Son, Jesus (John 3:16), and He still bestows love, mercy, and blessings upon us on a daily basis. When we align ourselves with God's heart, we automatically become more giving with our time, talents, love, and resources.

Being generous extends beyond money donations to include giving in all facets of one's life. It is about sharing the love, knowledge, and gifts that God has bestowed upon us. In Matthew 10:8, Jesus stated, "Freely you have received; freely give." Giving freely reflects God's heart and fosters an atmosphere in which benefits can come pouring in.

Recognizing that blessings multiply as one gives is one of the fundamental foundational ideas of being a distribution center. Like a seed sown in the land yielding a far larger harvest than the seed itself, so too can yield larger rewards. According to the Bible, "Give and you will receive." Luke 6:38 states, "A good measure, pressed down, shaken together, and running over, will be poured into your lap." This verse exemplifies the idea that when we give, God rewards us much more, making it possible for us to carry on rewarding other people.

The Peril of Ignoring Sacred Schedules

Although God intends for us to be channels through which He distributes His gifts, there is a serious risk that we will overlook this calling because of outside distractions and erroneous priorities. The guests in Luke 14:17–18 offered justifications for their decision to put their matters ahead of accepting the banquet invitation. Similarly, we might quickly lose sight of the heavenly chances God presents to us to be a benefit because we are preoccupied with our own lives.

Distractions can take many forms, such as pursuing wealth, relationships, success, or just day-to-day activities. These pursuits are not inherently wrong, but if we allow them to divert us from our ultimate goal, we give them the upper hand over God's plan. The visitors in the tale were only wrapped up in their worries; they were not indulging in any immoral behavior. But because they didn't reply to the invitation, they couldn't receive the blessings intended for them.

To avoid missing heavenly appointments, we need to have sensitive hearing and stay receptive to God's guidance. This necessitates praying, reading the Bible, and asking God to guide our lives. Even when He presents us with unexpected opportunities to be a blessing, we can identify them when tuned in to His Spirit.

The Benefits of Faithfulness and Obedience

God gives us more rewards and duties when we follow our mission to serve as distribution hubs. In Matthew 25:14–30, the parable of the talents describes how the servant who invested his master's money carefully received an even larger reward. This story shows us that God improves our ability to accept and give more when we are loyal to the resources He has given us, whether they be material, interpersonal, or spiritual.

It's crucial to remember, though, that compliance is essential to this process. It is not enough to be blessed alone; we also need to use our blessings according to God's instructions. Sometimes, God may ask us to give in ways that challenge or make us uncomfortable. He may ask us to give when we believe we don't have enough or to serve in areas where we feel unqualified. However, we put ourselves in a position to receive bigger gifts when we follow His guidance and step forth in trust.

Consistency is another aspect of faithfulness; it's not enough to merely give or serve when it's convenient; one must make generosity a way of life. A distribution center is a continuous activity that receives and distributes commodities continuously. In the same manner, no matter what season we are in, we are to always be willing to receive from God and give to others. As long as we stay true to God's calling, we can have assurance that He will provide for us, whether we are going through a period of plenty or testing.

Taking Up Positions for Overflow

If you want to become an actual distribution point for God's benefits, you must prepare yourself for overflow—a situation in which you are so full of God's kindness that it spontaneously pours out to others. This entails allowing God to bless you beyond your current necessities and lining your heart with His purposes.

Keeping an attitude of thankfulness is one approach to setting yourself up for overflow. When you express gratitude to God for what He has already given you, you allow more benefits to enter your life. By changing your attention from what you lack to what you have, gratitude fosters an environment of abundance where blessings can grow.

Stewardship is another essential to setting yourself up for overflow. Whether or not you can handle more depends on how you use the resources God has given you. God will trust you with more if you are loyal with what you have, including your time, money, and abilities. Being generous with what you have, no matter how little, is another aspect of stewardship. The widow who offered two little pennies in Mark 12:41–44 is a potent illustration of this idea. Despite the fact that her gift appeared modest, Jesus claimed that she donated more than anybody else because she trusted God to supply despite her poverty.

Steering Clear of the Selfish and Greed Pitfalls

God wants to bless us, but he also warns against letting greed and selfishness rule our lives. When a distribution center hoards products instead of distributing them, it can no longer serve its intended role. In the same manner, we lose the chance to be used by God to help others when we become unduly preoccupied with obtaining riches or blessings for ourselves.

Jesus counseled His disciples to store up treasures in heaven rather than on earth, where rust and moth devour everything (Matthew 6:19–20). This implies

that using our riches to further God's kingdom and bless others should be our main priority rather than accumulating material belongings.

Furthermore, greed might cause us to lose sight of blessings' actual purpose. When we see blessings as a way to fulfill our needs, we become victims of materialism and consumerism. But when we realize that benefits are meant to be shared, we find the fulfillment and joy that come from being a channel for God's love and support.

CHAPTER 5

MOVING FROM APPETIZERS TO THE MAIN COURSE

Many individuals find themselves skipping the main course—the entirety of God's intentions and purposes—in life in favor of the appetizers and fleeting glimpses of His provision. God's blessings frequently appear gradually, and although the first signs are amazing, they are not supposed to be the last. These are only the first steps. To avoid settling for less when the better is still on the way, we will examine how to discern between God's appetizers and His main meal in this chapter.

As stated in Matthew 22:14 TPT, the chapter's major text, "For everyone is invited to enter in, but few respond in excellence." This gets right to the core of the issue: while many are invited to partake in all that God has prepared, only a tiny percentage of people respond in a way that makes this possible. Many people accept less because they mistakenly believe that the preliminary indications of God's provision will eventually materialize, missing out on the bigger things that God has in store.

The Phases of Divine Supply

To escape the trap of settling for less, we must realize that God's provision frequently occurs in phases. Similar to a multicourse dinner, the appetizer is merely a tiny taste of what's to come and not the main part. Similar to this, God's early blessings on us are not supposed to be the conclusion of the story. They provide us a sample of what He has in store, which is much more.

In the Bible, we discover many examples of people who experienced God's provision in phases. Consider the Israelites as an example. God met their urgent needs in the wilderness by sending them manna from heaven each day (Exodus 16:4). Although this daily supply was extraordinary and more than enough in the short term, it did not represent the entirety of God's promise. There was still the Promised Land, flowing with honey and milk, the main course. But many of the Israelites forgot the bigger promise that awaited and grew accustomed to the manna, longing to return to Egypt (Numbers 11:5–6).

If you just eat the appetizers, you run the risk of growing accustomed to the brief fix and losing sight of the bigger picture. God wants us to understand that even though He provides for our immediate needs, if we keep walking in trust and obedience, He still has much more in store for us.

Mistaking the Main Course for the Appetizer

People often confuse appetizers for the main course, one reason they cannot fully appreciate God's benefits. Little triumphs, early accomplishments, and early discoveries are thrilling and can seem to represent the completion of God's purpose. But these are just hors d'oeuvres, little tasters of things to come.

This occurs when we lose sight of the bigger picture because we are too preoccupied with the current provision. For instance, it's simple to believe, "This is it!," when God grants you a new job, financial breakthrough, or relationship restoration. I've reached my intended location. These advantages, however, are merely the beginning. God has you ready for something far greater.

Keeping your focus on God's ultimate plan for your life is the key to avoiding this error. All of God's blessings and provisions along the journey are intended to equip you for the more important work to which God has called you. The danger arises in being complacent or happy with the appetizer, thinking that you have arrived while, in fact, the main meal is still on its way.

Answering the Call for Greater Things

Jesus discusses the offer to better things in Matthew 22:14, saying that "everyone is invited to enter in, but few respond in excellence." According to this text, many people are encouraged to share in the abundance of God's blessings, but very few truly behave in a way that makes it possible for them to do so.

What does it mean to give an excellent response? It implies that you hold on to all that God has offered. It implies you keep going after the initial blessings because you know God will do something more significant. It also means that you connect your life with God's purpose and are prepared to wait for His perfect timing.

It takes trust and persistence to respond to requests with excellence. You must be able to persevere when it would be easier to give up and accept the lesser blessings and have faith that God has more in store for you even when you can't see it yet. It's simple to get used to the appetizer, especially if it satisfies your immediate needs, but God invites us to focus on the main course, which is the entirety of His plan.

The Peril of Accepting Less

One of the most significant risks we take in our spiritual journey is settling for less than God intended. This occurs when we lose sight of God's more excellent plan for our life and grow satiated with the little favors. There are several causes of settling for less:

Impatience: We anticipate instant results in a world that moves quickly. When God's promises take longer than anticipated to materialize, we tend to get content with what we already have, believing that the bigger good might never arrive. We become impatient and quit waiting for the main entrée in favor of grabbing the appetizer.

Comfort: Because it offers stability and comfort, there are moments when the appetizer seems sufficient. We grow accustomed to the little gifts in life, and the idea of going after something bigger seems needless or dangerous. But being in our comfort zones can keep us from experiencing all that God has in store for us.

Fear of Disappointment: We may choose to accept less out of fear of having our hopes raised and not being met. We believe settling for the appetizer is safer than the whole course, so we lower our expectations. However, God commands us to live by faith, putting our trust in His ability to keep His word.

Lack of Vision: We are more prone to accept the lesser benefits if we don't have a clear picture of the bigger things God has in store. Our vision provides us with the drive to keep moving forward by keeping our attention on the end result. We are more prone to accept what is in front of us if we lack vision.

Recognizing God's Bigger Plan

We need to develop a mindset that acknowledges the phases of God's provision and maintains focus on His larger plan to resist settling for less. This calls for discernment—the capacity to tell the difference between the appetizers and the entrée. By exercising discernment, we can focus on the bigger picture while still appreciating the little things in life.

Maintaining a spiritual connection with God through prayer and Bible study is one approach to develop discernment. The better we know His heart and His promises, the more we can discern when He is calling us to something more. **God has good intentions for us, plans to prosper rather than harm us, and plans to offer us hope and a future, as Jeremiah 29:11 reminds us.** This knowledge gives us the confidence to keep moving forward, even when the appetizers look satisfying.

To accept God's larger plan, we also need to be prepared to give up our ambitions and aspirations. Occasionally, the appetizers look good, and we might be tempted to accept them as they satisfy our needs or preferences. Nevertheless, God's plan is always superior to our own. When we submit to His will, we make room for the main course—the abundance of His provision.

Pursuing the Fullness of God's Blessings

It takes an active pursuit of God's presence and promises to pursue the fullness of His benefits. It is insufficient only to accept the appetizers and then give up on getting more. We have to keep seeking God's will for our life, believing that He has bigger plans for us.

According to the Bible, God's power at work inside us allows Him to do immeasurably more than we could ever ask or imagine (Ephesians 3:20). This implies that the main meal will always be much better than we could have ever imagined, regardless of how delicious the appetizer appears to be. We can never fully comprehend God's benefits, but when we follow His plan in its entirety, we put ourselves in a position to receive more than we could have ever imagined.

CHAPTER 6

UNDERSTANDING YOUR DIVINE CALLING

I t is simple to become disoriented in a world where social pressure, diversions, and the need to fit in are all present. Yet, every person created by God has a divine calling—an individual destiny intricately woven into the fabric of God's vast design. Examining this concept will help you see how embracing your divine calling is crucial to making a difference and shining the light of Christ in your life and the world around you.

Before you were born, God knew you.

The Bible demonstrates that God has a specific and deliberate purpose for us. God addresses the prophet in Jeremiah 1:5 (TPT), saying, "I knew you before I formed you in the womb; I set you apart; I appointed you as a prophet to the nations." This remark holds great significance as it discloses that God has a plan for our lives even before birth. He has thoughtfully created a goal that aligns with His kingdom and will.

Understanding that our skills, aptitudes, or credentials do not determine this calling is critical. Its foundation is found in God's omniscience and sovereignty. Many people devote years to pursuing goals, aspirations, or dreams that would make their lives meaningful, but in the end, true fulfillment and purpose can only be found in following God's divine calling.

Recognizing God's Intent for Your Life

Finding God's calling starts with a heart willing to be devoted to His pursuit. This frequently means putting aside your goals and aspirations to focus on learning what God wants to do through you. The procedure isn't always straightforward because it requires patience, trust, and an open mind to follow the Holy Spirit's guidance.

A common misconception among believers is that their divine calling necessitates a large-scale ministry or international recognition. But each person's calling from God is distinct. Being a responsible worker, a kind friend, a devoted parent, or a leader in the community church are some examples of how it could appear. Even if God's calling may not seem like anyone else's, it is just as significant and vital in His kingdom. The secret is to hear what He has to say, recognize the particular area of your life where He is calling you to shine, and be prepared to accept that call.

Why Make a Declaration Is Crucial to Achieving Your Divine Destiny?

People tend to link being unique with being noticed, becoming well-known, or obtaining popularity. However, in God's kingdom, being noticeable entails leading a life that honors Him. You become more unique from the world around you as you align with God's plan for your life. **Matthew 5:14 (TPT) states, "You are the world's light."** A city perched on a hill cannot be concealed. Our calling as Christians is to be unique, not to fit in. We must beam our light and brighten the dark regions.

Being different just for being different is not what it means to stand out for God. Instead, it's about living according to His Word, obeying His direction, and letting His light illuminate everything we do. This frequently entails choosing to live by God's standards, even when it's uncomfortable or unpopular, and rejecting the patterns of the world.

Many people fail to realize their divine destiny because they are preoccupied with fitting in or taking the road of least resistance.

They make the compromise of leading a secure and ordinary existence out of fear of rejection or criticism. However, God's calling aims to raise you above the ordinary. You have to step out in trust and have confidence that God will give you the resources you need for the trip ahead.

Spiritual Readiness: Taking the Center Stage

Spiritual preparation is necessary before you can fully embrace your divine calling. It is unheard of for God to call the unprepared or the reluctant. Scripture is replete with examples of people whom God called to greatness but who had to undergo a period of preparation before being called.

Consider the tale of David, the shepherd lad who received a kingly call. **1 Samuel 16:11–13 (MSG) describes the occasion of David's kingship inauguration by Samuel.** However, David spent years caring for sheep, growing in humility, and strengthening his faith in God before he held the throne. David's heart was formed in the fields, far from prying eyes for the part he would play.

Similarly, Esther prepared for an extended period before ascending to the throne and saving her people. **Before being introduced to the king, Esther 2:12 (TPT) details how she and the other women underwent a year of beauty treatments.** This was a time of spiritual and emotional preparation for the critical role that Esther would play, in addition to physical preparation.

Patience and endurance are typically required during preparation. It can be easy to want the limelight before God has given us what we need. But God has perfect timing, and He knows what we must learn to stand out the way He wants us to. If you find yourself in a season of preparation, don't detest it. Trust that God is using this time to refine your skills, grow your faith, and develop your character.

The Price of Pursuing Your Sacred Calling

It's crucial to remember that pursuing your spiritual calling involves expenses. "Whoever wants to be my disciple must deny themselves and take up their cross daily and follow me," says Jesus

Himself in Luke 9:23 (TPT). Standing out comes with a cost, and that cost is frequently sacrificed.

Consider the rich young ruler in Matthew 19:21 (MSG). He asked Jesus what he had to do to be granted eternal life, and Jesus said, "Go sell everything you own and give it all to the poor if you want to give it all you have. Then, all of your possessions will be in heaven. Come with me, then. The young man missed his chance to stand out and pursue Christ's higher calling because he couldn't bring himself to make that sacrifice.

Similarly, God may require you to give up anything, be it stability, comfort, or personal goals, to accomplish His plan for your life. However, God will always multiply back to you in ways you cannot fathom, no matter what you sacrifice for Him.

Leading a Life That Glorifies God

Ultimately, leading a life that exalts God is what it means to embrace your divine calling. When you align yourself with His purpose, you become a vessel through which His power and grace can flow. Others will be drawn to the light within you and directed toward Christ as you blaze forth and stand out.

In Philippians 2:15 (TPT), the apostle Paul expressed his understanding when he wrote, "Leave a cheerful life, without complaining or division among yourselves." Because even though you live in a cruel and perverted civilization, you will be seen as the pure, innocent children of God. Because you will be seen among them as bright lights in the cosmos. Your spiritual calling is intended to affect everyone around you, not just yourself. When you live out your calling, you brighten the planet's darkest corners and give those in need comfort, healing, and the truth.

Answer the Call, Make an Impact, and Shine Brightly

It's time for each of us to accept God's unique calling. This calling involves more than merely drawing attention to ourselves; it involves using the purpose that God has given each of us. By using spiritual readiness, selflessness, and a readiness to submit to His plan, we can enter the limelight that God has intended for us.

Recall that you were intended for this exact moment in time. You, too, have been called for a particular purpose, just as Esther was called to save her people, David to be king, and Paul to be an apostle. This is your chance to make an impression, shine brightly, and use your life to exalt God.

CHAPTER 7

THE POWER OF SACRIFICE AND OBEDIENCE

The two things essential to our spiritual journey that consistently bring God's favor and benefits are obedience and sacrifice. These two concepts are closely related because faithful obedience frequently requires sacrifice and because sacrifice is meaningless without obedience. Giving up something allows us to get higher spiritual things that God has in store for us, whether it be money, possessions, time, or personal preferences. But fundamentally, these sacrifices are meaningful because of their obedience, which also pleases God. 1 Samuel 15:22 (TPT) reminds us that obedience is better than sacrifice. This chapter explores the need for sacrifice and obedience in our relationship with God, emphasizing how these elements complement one another to bring about heavenly benefits and accomplish His promises.

The Focus on Sacrifice in the Bible

The Bible is replete with instances demonstrating how sacrifices are necessary to obtain more blessings. Scripture shows how God uses sacrifice to try, refine, and prepare His people to fulfill His promises. Giving up something valuable to accomplish something more is the essence of sacrifice. It is an expression of faith in God's providence and plan, knowing that the benefits He will bring will much outweigh the little setbacks.

In the Old Testament, the relationship between God and His people depended on offerings. These gifts, which can be food, animals, or other offerings, fulfilled two purposes: acts of worship and atonement. However, as 1 Samuel 15:22 makes evident, merely sacrificing is insufficient. The only way that sacrifice can be fully appreciated is via obedience, which is why God desires a heart that submits to Him. This idea is illustrated by the story of King Saul, who disobeyed God by retaining the finest animals during a military conquest to present them as a sacrifice. However, God rejected Saul's offering as it was founded on disobedience, emphasizing that sacrifice is incomplete without obedience.

The Importance of Offering in Obtaining God's Favor

To fully understand God's promises, we must admit that often, the way to unlock them involves sacrifice. Sacrifice requires more than just giving things up; it also entails making space for God's more incredible blessings. Releasing yourself from earthly bonds, such as comfort, ambitions, or financial possessions, demonstrates our faith in God's ability to provide something far better.

One of the most important examples is Abraham, who was willing to offer his only son, Isaac, as a sacrifice in answer to God's command. In Genesis 22, God tests Abraham's faith by asking him to present Isaac as a burnt offering. It must have been an agonizing request, yet Abraham complied without question. God intervened and provided a ram to replace Abraham's son as a sacrifice, just as he raised the knife to offer him. Abraham was willing to give up what was most essential to him, demonstrating his commitment and faith in God. God, therefore, lavishly benefited Abraham. Abraham became the father of many nations due to his descendants inheriting God's covenant promises.

Abraham teaches us that blessings usually follow sacrifice. Sometimes God tests our faith and preparation for the greater things He has in store for us by asking us to give up the things we cherish most. We sacrifice because we believe that God's methods are higher than ours and that His thoughts are higher than ours (Isaiah 55:9). When we are ready to give up our desires to further God's kingdom, He accepts our giving and works through His promises in ways we can never imagine.

The Way to Greater Blessings via Obedience

Even while sacrifice has excellent power, obedience finally allows God's blessings to be fully experienced. The Bible makes it quite evident that obedience is what God values most. Being obedient involves more than just observing the law; it also involves trusting God and aligning our emotions with His will. It necessitates humility and a readiness to yield to His authority, especially when unsure of His intentions.

King Saul's fall from grace in 1 Samuel 15 is a prime illustration of how disobedience can deprive us of God's favor. God commanded Saul to wipe out all the Amalekites and everything they owned, but he chose to rescue the best animals and brought them back as war booty. When confronted by the prophet Samuel, Saul attempted to defend his actions by saying that he planned to offer the livestock as sacrifices to God. However, Samuel's reply was unambiguous: 1 Samuel 15:22: "To obey is better than sacrifice, and to heed is better than the fat of rams." Saul's partial obedience —what appeared like a tiny compromise—ultimately lost him his reign. We can learn from this narrative that obedience has no short routes. When God gives us an instruction, we must obey it without question or justification.

Faithful obedience frequently entails sacrifice, yet it is precisely via this obedience that we set ourselves up to be showered with God's best. **"Trust in the Lord completely, and do not rely on your own opinions," reads Proverbs 3:5–6 (TPT).** Put all your trust in him to lead you; he will assist you in your decisions. We show our faith in God's plan when we obey Him, even when it's challenging or makes no sense. God can now guide us into more enormous rewards and opportunities that we would never be able to access on our own because of our confidence in him.

Identifying the Distinction Between the "Main Course" and the "Appetizer"

Being able to distinguish between what is transient and what is permanent is one of the biggest obstacles to walking in obedience and sacrifice. In God's plan, there are times when He provides us with what could appear to be instant benefits—an "appetizer," if you will—but these are merely a taste of the more substantial blessings. There's a risk involved in opting for the appetizer rather than the main course.

For instance, in the Genesis 25 account of Esau and Jacob, Esau gave up his birthright for a bowl of stew out of weakness. As the firstborn, Esau received a material and spiritual blessing. This was his birthright. However, Esau gave up the eternal for the transient out of hunger. This tale exemplifies how quickly we can become distracted from God's more significant promises when we let our short-term wants or needs take precedence over the long-term benefits He has in store.

Using discernment is the key to avoiding these pitfalls. We must be able to tell the difference between the fleeting benefits the world provides and the everlasting benefits of doing what God commands. Sacrifice is frequently required because it lets us let go of the "appetizers" and create a place for God's planned "main course. " Obedience is the method to ensure we don't accept anything less than what God has planned for us.

Biblical Illustrations of Obedience and Sacrifice

The Bible is replete with people who made a lasting impression by being prepared to give their all to serve God's kingdom. These men and women are potent examples of what it means to follow God with all your heart and enjoy the benefits of doing so.

As was already revealed, Abraham was prepared to offer his son

Isaac as a sacrifice to God. His narrative shows no sacrifice is too big to accomplish God's will. Abraham's faith and obedience made it possible for future generations to benefit from God's covenant blessings in addition to him.

Another person who gave up her safety to defend God's people is Esther. Esther put herself in danger when she approached the king without being called, a move that would have resulted in her death as a Jewish queen in a strange country. However, she decided to heed God's summons to pray for her people, stating, "If I perish, I perish" (Esther 4:16). Esther proved the value of obedience in the face of extreme danger by being willing to give up her life and status, which ultimately resulted in the deliverance of the Jewish people.

Lastly, we cannot ignore Jesus Christ, the ultimate example of obedience and sacrifice.

"Not my will, but yours be done" was Jesus' prayer in the Garden of Gethsemane (Luke 22:42). He voluntarily gave His life to the Father's plan for human redemption. Because of His obedience, redemption, and eternal life are now possible for everyone who believes in Jesus. His offering is a living example of the adage that the most excellent obedience results in the greatest blessings.

The Eternal Overcomes the Temporary

Obedience and sacrifice are essential components of the Christian life. Although they are complex and frequently expensive, the benefits never fade. God holds us to a higher standard in a culture where seeking personal pleasure and rapid gratification are valued more highly than laying down our lives, our wants, and our plans to submit to His perfect will.

When we accept the power of obedience and sacrifice, we put ourselves in a position to benefit from God's most significant rewards. We experience the fullness of His promises in ways beyond anything the world has to offer, and we can distinguish between the transient and the eternal.

CHAPTER 8

STEPPING INTO GREATER REALMS OF RESPONSIBILITY

More authority in the Kingdom of God frequently translates into more fulfillment, influence, and impact. Similar to what Matthew 25:21 (TPT) says, "I will set you over much because you have been faithful over a little." This concept applies to any believer who dares to follow the divine calling that has been put on their life. Assuming more responsibility is more than just aiming for status or power; it means excelling in life by achieving God's distinct purpose for each of us and shining brightly in a world full of darkness.

In this chapter, we will examine the important relationship between accountability and growth in God's Kingdom. David's journey from shepherd kid to king will teach us valuable lessons. We'll also discuss how to face anxiety and uncertainty when God invites us to assume more responsibility. In the end, we'll find that accepting accountability is the first step toward a more meaningful future and a lively religious expression.

The Connection in God's Kingdom Between Promotion and Responsibility

Mature spiritual development and development depend on

accountability. When we take on greater responsibility, we demonstrate that we are ready for development in God's Kingdom. Similar to the parable of the talents in Matthew 25, where enslaved people were given varying amounts based on their capacities, we are allocated duties based on our faithfulness and capacity.

In this parable, the master shows that those obedient in small things will be trusted with greater ones by praising the enslaved people who utilized their talents correctly. We can incorporate this concept of loyalty into our everyday lives in modest ways. God is monitoring how we handle the responsibilities we already have, whether at home, in our ministries, or at work. Our commitment to serve and be diligent with what we have been given often determines the level of influence and opportunities God grants us in the future.

As we take on more responsibility, we set ourselves up for advancement and act as an example and source of inspiration for others. When we step up to the plate, others take note, and our readiness may inspire others to follow suit. Growing together, we create a culture of excellence and encourage others to assume their responsibilities in God's Kingdom, leading to a cascade of advancement and responsibility.

Lessons from David's Journey: From Shepherd to King

David's journey from a meek shepherd to the King of Israel is among the most inspiring tales of ascending to higher positions of authority. David's life serves as evidence that accepting responsibility frequently entails hardships, adjustments, and metamorphosis.

While David was still a little shepherd lad taking care of his father's sheep, he was crowned king. His future destiny was promised by the anointing, but it was not without difficulties. David was not crowned king right away; rather, he was thrown into a number of duties that put his faith, willpower, and character to the test.

Faithfulness in the Ordinary:

Before David faced the giant Goliath, he spent years in the fields, protecting his flock from lions and bears. It was during these quiet moments of tending sheep that David learned essential lessons about leadership, courage, and reliance on God. His faithfulness in these seemingly insignificant tasks prepared him for the greater challenges ahead. When the moment came to confront Goliath, David declared in **1 Samuel 17:37 (TPT)**, "The Lord who rescued me from the claws of the lion and the bear will rescue me from this Philistine!" David's faith and experience in the mundane had equipped him for monumental responsibilities.

Embracing Challenges:

When David defeated Goliath, he did not immediately ascend to the throne. Instead, he became a leader in King Saul's army, gaining fame and popularity. However, with this newfound responsibility came jealousy and challenges. Saul, feeling threatened by David's rising prominence, sought to kill him. David faced immense pressure and fear, yet he continued to fulfill his responsibilities as a soldier and leader. He did not retaliate against Saul; instead, he honored his king and trusted in God's timing.

David's journey teaches us that embracing greater responsibilities can often lead to difficult circumstances. It is not uncommon to face opposition, fear, or doubt when stepping into a new role. But it's only by overcoming these obstacles that we develop the kind of character required to lead successfully.

The Value of Personality:

David's time spent in the desert while escaping Saul helped to shape his personality. Despite his anointing, he discovered how to rely on God, ask for His direction, and maintain his humility. In the end, his patience, devotion to God, and loyalty brought him to the throne of Israel. Once he was crowned king, he realized how important it was to govern with honesty and loyalty and how much responsibility that came with the job.

David's experience reminds us that accepting more responsibility frequently means facing challenges and holding fast to our beliefs. God shapes us into the leaders He wants us to be through these experiences, preparing us for the work that lies ahead.

Overcoming Fear and Doubt When God Puts You in Charge of More Important Tasks

Many of us experience anxiety and uncertainty when confronted with new duties, even in the face of the possibility of advancement and the examples of obedient leaders like David. It might be frightening to consider moving outside our comfort zones, and our fear of failing keeps us from accepting God's responsibilities.

Acknowledging Your Fears:

The first step in overcoming fear is acknowledging its presence. It's normal to feel apprehensive when facing greater responsibilities. Fear can manifest in various forms: fear of inadequacy, failure, or the unknown. However, we must remember that God does not call the equipped; He equips the called. Our worries can indicate where we need to grow in faith.

Accepting the Promises of God:

When God asks us to assume more responsibility, our hearts must be rooted in His promises. God comforts us in Isaiah 41:10 (TPT), saying, "Do not yield to fear, for I am always near." I am your devoted God; never take your eyes off of me. I'll pour my strength into you and support you no matter what. This assurance is a reminder that God is with us and will provide us with the strength and direction we need to succeed in our duties.

Looking for Advice and Assistance:

Seeking help and direction from others is crucial when venturing into more responsible areas. Having spiritual leaders, mentors, and like-minded people around us can give us the motivation we need to face our fears. Furthermore, prayer and seeking God's guidance can help us discern our calling and overcome obstacles.

Making Tiny Faith-Based Steps:

Often, taking baby steps toward faith is what it takes to overcome fear. Divide the responsibilities into smaller, more doable tasks rather than dwelling on how big they are. Every little act of obedience increases our self-assurance and shows how dedicated we are to answering God's call. God will meet us in our obedience as we follow these steps, giving us the strength to take on more responsibility.

Believing in God's Autonomy:

Lastly, we have to have faith in God's omnipotence. He is aware of His purposes for us, and they are full of hope and meaning (Jeremiah 29:11). God is in control, so we don't need to worry when we face challenges or feel overpowered. He has given us all we require to be successful in our duties, and His grace is enough to meet whatever obstacle we encounter.

The Exhortation to Be Brilliant and Outstanding

As we advance in the Kingdom of God, we must take on increasingly significant responsibilities. When we accept the tasks placed before us, we put ourselves in a position for advancement, influence, and fulfillment. Our determination to overcome more significant obstacles can result in amazing rewards and chances to shine forth for God's glory, just as David's path tells us.

We are expected to be different in a society that frequently avoids taking on responsibilities. It is our duty to overcome uncertainty and fear by accepting the roles that others might shun. As we assume our duties, we become change agents in our communities and abroad, reflecting the light of Christ.

In the hope that God would reward us greatly for our faithfulness in the small things, let us make an effort to be good stewards of the duties entrusted to us. We will accomplish our divine destiny and make a difference in the world for God's Kingdom if we answer the call to shine and excel.

CHAPTER 9

ALIGNING WITH GOD'S TIMING AND PLAN

T he concept of timing is one of the most important things we have to negotiate in our journey through life and faith. The author profoundly says, "He has made everything beautiful in its time," in Ecclesiastes 3:11 (TPT). By realizing this, we may align ourselves with God's perfect timing and discern the times when we are being set up for something bigger.

For every believer, patience and discernment are vital qualities in a world that frequently wants instant results and easy solutions. The significance of waiting for God's appointed time and the perils of settling for less than what He has in store will be discussed in this chapter. Esther's tale will teach us how following God's timing can lead to success, authority, and major breakthroughs.

Identifying Sacred Times of Advancement and Discovery

When pursuing our purpose and destiny, God's timing is crucial. Scripture is replete with instances of divine moments in which God steps in and uses people to further His purposes. It takes spiritual insight, knowledge of God's nature, and a dedication to patient prayer to recognize these times.

The Value of Holding Out:

Of the most difficult parts of our spiritual journeys can be waiting. It frequently puts our endurance, tenacity, and faith in God to the test. But waiting is an active act of faith; it is not a passive one. Waiting on God puts us in a position to recognize His voice and understand His purposes. **"This is what I've learned through it all: Don't give up; don't be impatient; be entwined as one with the Lord," encourages Psalm 27:14 (TPT).** Have guts and bravery, and never give up hope. Yes, don't give up waiting; He won't let you down.

We allow God the chance to work out the details of our life in ways that are beyond our comprehension when we wait, trusting in His perfect timing. Although the waiting period may seem like a silent season, it is frequently a moment of preparation, refining, and divine timing.

Recognizing Heavenly Occasions:

Opportunities or changes in circumstances are frequently the manifestations of divine moments of elevation and breakthrough. They could show up as a job opportunity, an unexpected encounter, or a prayer-inspired discovery. It is imperative that we continue to be aware of these instances and ask God for guidance in determining what He wants.

For example, we can observe how Esther's location and timing were essential for her people's deliverance in the story. Esther's elevation to queen was not plain coincidence; it was divinely ordained. She knew that she had to act quickly when it came time to confront King Xerxes. She realized that her role was to ensure her people's salvation as well as her own.

Prayer's Significance in Timing:

Prayer is essential to align ourselves with God's timing. We ask for His direction, learn about His purposes, and find the fortitude to wait in the private chamber of prayer. James 1:5 (TPT) reminds us that "whoever desires wisdom, ask God for it, and He will grant it." We can discover God's perfect time by praying and knowing when to act and when to remain motionless.

Before she approached the king, Esther urged her people to fast and pray for three days. Through her prayer, she not only asked divine intervention for the hardship she was about to face, but also aligned her heart with God's plan. face. Her readiness to act in faith, coupled with her understanding of timing, ultimately led to her elevation as a key player in her people's deliverance.

The Peril of Achieving Less Than What God Is Up to

We must resist the need to accept less than what God has planned for us while we work to line up with His timeline. Life's stresses, social pressures, and fear of the unknown can cause us to make snap decisions and break the commitments God has given us.

The Allure of Instant Satisfaction:

In a society where accomplishments are frequently rewarded quickly, getting caught up in the trap of wanting satisfaction right now is simple. We might discover that, although they appear advantageous at the time, we end up sidetracking God's bigger purpose.

In this sense, The story of Abraham and Hagar serves as a warning. Abraham and Sarah were frustrated and made their own plan after waiting for God's promise of a son for years. They went to Hagar, which had grave repercussions. They chose to act before God's appointed time, which led to discord and struggle, rather than waiting for His perfect timing.

God has prepared rewards for us, but we run the danger of losing them when we accept less than His finest. Our impatience can cause us to take actions that are contrary to His plan, which will ultimately cause His promises to be delayed in our lives.

Accepting the Promises of God:

Remaining firm in faith and putting your trust in God's promises is essential to aligning with His timing. We may wait for God's timing with confidence when we accept His promises. We are urged to adhere firmly to the hope that resides within us because God consistently fulfills His promises in Hebrews 10:23 (TPT).

Esther's journey serves as an example of this. She was overcome with a great deal of worry and doubt when Mordecai pushed her to talk to the king about preserving their people. She did, however, decide to line herself up with God's plan and the current circumstances. God's destiny for her people was eventually fulfilled and she was promoted as a result of her willingness to take a risk in faith.

Esther's Submission to Divine Timing: Advancement and Power

Esther's narrative serves as a wonderful example of how important it is to follow God's schedule and will. As an orphan, Esther ended up in Xerxes' royal court, where she eventually rose to the position of queen. But there was a reason for her position that went well beyond her luxury and pleasure.

Positioning Divinely:

Esther's accession to the throne was a divine appointment for a pivotal historical event. Esther played a special role when a plan to exterminate the Jewish people was discovered. Her timing was perfect; she found herself in a position to persuade the monarch and rescue her people.

Having the guts to recognize this magnificent moment was necessary. Esther was in danger of being called upon when she went to see the king without being invited. Nevertheless, she saw the gravity of her duty and positioned herself in accordance with God's schedule. "If you keep quiet during this time, liberation and rescue will arise for the Jews from another place, but you and your family will perish," Mordecai cautions her in Esther 4:14 (TPT). Who knows, maybe this is the moment you were crowned queen."

Esther's answer demonstrates how in line with God's plan she is. Choosing to use her position for the greater good, she made the decision to act in faith. Her readiness to fulfill her role at the right moment led to her advancement, power, and her people's deliverance.

The Ability to Discern:

Esther's path also demonstrates the value of discernment in appreciating God's timing. Instead of making a snap decision, she took the time to pray and ask for guidance. Through prayer and fasting, she obtained the strength and clarity to approach the king strategically.

Using judgment is essential when making big decisions in our lives. We have to seek God's wisdom and pay attention to what the Holy Spirit says. Our hearts become one with His, and we are able to discern those holy moments of breakthrough and elevation.

Recognizing God's Absolute Power:

In the end, Esther's tale serves as a reminder of God's omnipotence in carrying out His purposes. God is active even in the face of terrible situations. By having faith in His timing and power, we can confidently face the obstacles we face in life.

God is working everything out for our benefit, so long as we line ourselves with His timing (Romans 8:28). It is our responsibility to continue being obedient, watchful, and perceptive while believing He will create beauty in His time.

Putting the Higher Goal First

Complying with God's will and schedule is a crucial part of our spiritual path. We must resist the urge to accept anything less than what God has planned for us while we look for signs of divine moments of exaltation. Esther's story is a potent reminder that we can achieve promotion, authority, and great breakthroughs if we are ready to align with God's timing.

We are called to embrace patience and discernment in a world that frequently places a premium on instant results. We prepare ourselves for the bigger picture that God has in store when we wait on Him and ask for His guidance. According to Ecclesiastes 3:11, "He has made everything beautiful in its time," we are reminded. May we put our faith in His perfect time, daring to enter the roles He has for us, and radiating His glory.

Let us be alert in seeking God's will and cognizant of the holy moments He reveals as we consider our own lives. Together, we can learn to appreciate the wonder of waiting and the significant benefits of lining up with God's ideal timing.

CHAPTER 10

PROPHETIC UTTERANCES AND PRAYER SESSIONS

Prophetic Utterance for the Month:

- "This is a month of divine speed. God is accelerating His purposes in your life. What has been delayed is being released suddenly. You will testify of swift and supernatural breakthroughs."

- "Doors that seemed permanently closed are opening this month. You will walk into opportunities that you never imagined. It is a season of favor and divine appointments."

- "There is a shift in the spiritual atmosphere. Chains of delay, hindrance, and stagnation are broken. You are moving forward into the fullness of God's promises for your life."

- "Prepare for unexpected visitations from the Lord. Angelic interventions are being released to bring forth the manifestation of what has been prophesied over you."

Prophetic Declaration Over Finances:

- "This is the season where God is visiting your finances. Expect financial breakthrough from unexpected sources. Resources that were once blocked are now being released."

- "There is a breaking of financial limitations. You will not lack. God is causing your storehouse to overflow as you align with His principles of giving and sowing."

- "Financial debts will be supernaturally erased. Divine strategies for wealth creation are being imparted to you now."

Prophetic Utterance for Families:

- "Family reconciliation is happening this season. Estranged relationships are being healed and restored by the power of God."

- "Your family will experience divine protection and provision. The storms that have raged are being calmed by the Prince of Peace."

- "Household salvation is coming to pass. Family members who have strayed will return to God, and new levels of spiritual growth are being ignited in your home."

Prophetic Utterance for Health and Healing:

- "This month marks the end of chronic illnesses and long-term health challenges. Healing is your portion, and it will manifest suddenly."

- "God is releasing healing angels to touch areas of your body that have been afflicted. Expect supernatural recovery and strength to return."

- "What medical professionals could not solve; God is resolving by His mighty hand. You will be a living testimony of divine healing."

Prophetic Utterance Over Nations:

- "There will be a shifting in the leadership of nations. God is raising leaders who will bring righteousness and justice. Corrupt systems are being exposed and overthrown."

- "Nations will witness sudden revival. A hunger for the things of God is spreading, and there will be an unprecedented move of the Holy Spirit, drawing multitudes to salvation."

- "God's hand is intervening in conflicts and wars. Peace treaties will be signed, and restoration will come to war-torn regions as the Church rises to pray and intercede."

Prophetic Word Concerning Ministries and Callings:

- "Ministries are entering into their season of expansion and growth. New territories are being claimed for the Kingdom, and there will be an increase in influence."

- "Prophetic gifts are being stirred up. God is releasing a fresh prophetic mantle on His people to speak life, declare His Word, and shift atmospheres."

- "There will be divine connections and partnerships that will propel ministries to the next level. Be open to collaborate as God aligns His people for His purposes."

Prophetic Utterance for the Suddenly:

- "Suddenly, God will turn your mourning into dancing. What was lost will be restored sevenfold. Prepare for the sudden reversals in situations that seemed impossible."

- "You are stepping into your season of 'suddenly'—where long-standing prayers will be answered, and God will move in ways that will astonish you and those around you."

- "Be ready for divine surprises. This is the time for the unexpected to manifest. God is releasing His supernatural favor, and what should have taken years will be accomplished in days."

Prophetic Utterance on Favor:

- "This is the time to walk in unprecedented favor. The favor of God is resting on you, opening doors that no man can shut. Expect promotion and elevation."

- "Favor will surround you as a shield. As you go about your daily affairs, you will find people going out of their way to bless you, assist you, and support your endeavors."

- "The favor of God will cause your name to be mentioned in places of influence. God is positioning you for strategic relationships that will propel you into new realms."

Prayer Session

Prayer 1: Gratitude for God's Mercies and Grace

Father, in the Name of Jesus, by Your power and authority, by Your grace and mercy:

I thank You for Your mercies and grace.

I thank You for Your help over the past 5 months of this year, 2024.

I am grateful for the help of Your Spirit, for Your protection and preservation.

I am thankful for my growth, my spiritual experience, and my physical experience.

I am grateful for divine intervention, for frustrating the counsel of the enemy.

I thank You for defeating my foes and adversaries.

I thank You for victories and triumphs.

I am grateful for the battles I knew I fought and those I didn't know I fought.

I thank You for every victory. Take all the praise and glory.

In the Mighty Name of Jesus. *(Zechariah 4:6 TLB)*

Prayer 2: Thanksgiving for the First Five Months of the Year

Father, in the Name of Jesus, by Your power and authority, by Your grace and mercy:

I have returned to say thank you for the first five months of this great year.

I am grateful.

Thank you for the taste of victories.

Thank You for not allowing my enemies to laugh at me.

Thank you for not allowing my enemies to triumph over me and my family.

Thank You for not allowing the enemy to triumph over Church on Fire International.

Thank You for Your help, victory, and triumph.

Take all the glory.

In the Mighty Name of Jesus. *(Psalm 41:10-11 TLB/TPT)*

PRAYER 3: Adoration and Praise to God

Father, in the Name of Jesus, by Your power and authority, by Your grace and mercy:

My Father, I adore You; I admire You.

You are beautiful beyond description.

You are amazing, wonderful, and lovely.

Your lovingkindness is better than life to me.

My lips shall praise You, and I will sing to You.

I will bless You; I will lift up my hands to the holy hill and worship You.

O my Father, I praise You.

Thank you for the month of June.

I know all things are ready for me and my generation.

I am Your distributor and Your distribution center.

I am a distributor of Your goodness, favor, fortune, wealth, wisdom, and glory.

I will stream Your glory to my generation.

I adore You, I exalt You, I extol You, and I appreciate You.

I register my praise to You this month and in all that You are doing.

I receive all things that are ready so I can distribute them to my world.

Be glorified.

In the Name of Jesus. *(Psalm 34:1-3 TPT/MSG; Psalm 135:5,13 MSG)*

Prayer 4: Arresting and Declaring Over the Month of June

Father, in the Name of Jesus, by Your power and authority, by Your grace and mercy:

I arrest the month of June and declare that whatever is injected into this month by the enemy to hinder me, limit me, or rob me of greatness, by the power of the Holy Ghost, I eject you!

I reject every complication, contradiction, and negative reaction assigned against me, my household, Church on Fire International, and our loved ones.

I come against you by the power of the Holy Ghost.

I reject evil arrows, plots, agendas, and negative cycles.

I eject any wickedness that has been planted into this month by the power of the Holy Ghost.

I apply the redemptive power of the blood of Jesus.

I purge this month from every calamity, disaster, misfortune, and evil report.

Get out of the month of June!

I own this month, and it must respond to my destiny.

There must be angelic and heavenly intervention.

God will lift my head above my enemies.

Every power that seeks to bow my head in shame, you are paralyzed!

My head is lifted above my enemies, above shame and reproach.

I will hear and obey the voice of God.

- O my head, keep me ahead.

I command supernatural visibility, destiny reward, acknowledgment, and recognition.

I declare the month of June will lift me and skyrocket us to heights we will never recover from in glory and stardom.

We are roaring like warriors in the Name of Jesus. (*Deuteronomy 7:22 TLB; Matthew 13:7 TLB; Luke 1:26-40 AMP*)

Prayer 5: Declaring Favor and Breakthrough Over June

Father, in the Name of Jesus, by Your power and authority, by Your grace and mercy:

- O my head, reject any and every contradiction and complication.

This month of June is my month!

It's a different me, a new me, a powerful me, a favored me.

As the oil comes on me, I reject contradiction and complication and eject negativity.

- **In the Mighty Name of Jesus**. *(Luke 1:26-40 AMP)*

Prayer 6: Activation of Greatness Through the Oil of Anointing

Father, in the Name of Jesus, by Your power and authority, by Your grace and mercy:

- O oil, hear my voice and the voice of the Lord.

This time, I am in charge.

This matter of greatness belongs to me.

I will never be the shadow of my calling or destiny—it's impossible!

As You come upon my head, your assignment is to project and eject:

Project into my life every expectation for my life that is in the heart of God.

- Eject into my life every requirement that leads to commendation.

I will never be considered by God and rejected by God.

I will never be the one whose destiny is a shadow, nightmare, heartache, or rejection by my Heavenly Father.

O oil, project honor, favor, greatness, speed, achievement, protection, and preservation.

Inject into me surpassing intelligence, supernatural wisdom, skills needed, encouragement, guidance, revelations, and access to the throne of grace.

Above all, inject into me the ability to distribute the greatness of God to my generation.

Oil, you are now mandated to make me the champion that God will announce.

I am not a coward or a chameleon; I am a champion.

I am not a grasshopper; I am a giant and a giant killer.

I command the full manifestation of God's promises and honor.

I receive the unction to function beyond my capacity, expectation, and imagination.

I receive the unction to excel beyond the expectations of my enemies, mentors, and generation.

Let great men look at me and wonder at my greatness.

Let my name, life, and destiny align with God's greatness and advertise His glory and greatness.

PART

TWO

CHAPTER 11

INSTRUCTIONS FOR UNUSUAL LIFTING (PART A)

We must constantly overcome many struggles, obstacles, and tests in life. Every person has to intentionally work to elevate their spiritual, personal, and professional lives if they are to experience an unusual uplift.

Life may be compared to a game, as said in 2 Timothy 2:5 (KJV). Like any game, it has high stakes and requires strategy, dedication, and attention to succeed. This chapter will examine the critical areas where we must "step up" to experience the extraordinary elevation that God has planned for us.

Five Key 'Games' to Focus On:

1. Companionship and Individual Spiritual Life

All extraordinary liftings are based on our own relationship with God. When we consistently invite God into our daily lives through fellowship and devotion, His presence becomes more powerful and profound.

Psalm 63:1 emphasizes the importance of yearning for God's

presence every day. Our dedication and love for God are revealed in our daily interactions with Him. Personal devotion is the key to living a life of spiritual advancement. Without it, we are easily sidetracked, and our devotion to God wanes (Philippians 3:8 TPT).

Since he is aware that commitment is the key to your destiny, Satan will always want to sabotage it. Ecclesiastes 1:1–2 (KJV) says that although life is difficult, our devotion to God enables us to overcome these difficulties.

Do Not Forget These

Your personal devotion to God fuels your ardor, fervor, and zest for life. A persistent pursuit of God can help you maintain a strong spiritual foundation and be prepared for future challenges.

Due to a lack of personal devotion, small issues can seem like unbeatable obstacles, yet with God, even the most difficult obstacles become inconsequential (Numbers 13:33 TLB).

It will be easier for you to navigate life if others possess spiritual equipment as well. Surround yourself with people who know how to fight spiritual conflicts and are committed to their devotion to God.

2. Consistency in spiritual preparation

Because they do not take their spiritual preparation properly, a lot of people do not pass the exam of life. Just as students study hard for exams, we must also prepare for life's challenges by maintaining a firm spiritual foundation.

Do not forget these;

Regular spiritual preparation is essential for a remarkable ascent. Maintaining a relationship with God in the wilderness and the garden is more important than attending significant events.

Martin Luther reportedly said that he needed to pray for three hours a day just to keep up with his workload. This highlights the importance of prioritizing spiritual preparation in our everyday lives.

3. Acknowledging the Impact of Impartation

Unusual lifting can only be unlocked via impartation. Gifting increases elegance and sets you up for success. John 20:24–27 (TLB) emphasizes that people who miss out on spiritual events such as church services and others frequently do so because they are faithless and weak or often preoccupied with things outside their control.

Do Not Forget These;

Never let anything outside of yourself, such as faithlessness, weakness, or the existence or non-existence of a spiritual mentor, determine your spiritual path. Your purpose is too essential to be overlooked because of distractions, and your destiny is unique to you.

Impartation redresses spiritual imbalances and brings you into harmony with God's plan for your life.

4. A yearning for God's existence

You need to strongly desire God's presence if you wish to see an extraordinary rise. You will reach new spiritual heights and have a life-changing experience when you genuinely want to spend time alone with your Maker. God's anointing grows strong enough to cripple enemies and turn giants into bread in this realm of famine.

Do Not Forget These;

Even the most challenging obstacles become doable tasks with God on your side. But without God, even little issues grow into massive, overpowering difficulties (Numbers 14:2 TLB).

Create an environment where God's presence is paramount. Matthew 25:1-2 (TLB) states that those prepared with additional oil (spiritual preparation) can endure the difficulties ahead.

5. Create Trusted Bonds and Surround Yourself with Wonderful People

The more amazing people you have around you, the more greatness is nourished within and around you. Psalm 49:20 (KJV) reminds us that even with opportunity, one can end up needy without understanding and instruction. Be in the company of people who share your commitment to mental and spiritual development.

Do Not Forget These

According to Genesis 39:2 (KJV), true prosperity comes from the One who carries us, not from other sources like a job or status.

God's anointing and the presence of good counsel can change your life. They will open doors and propel you to new heights of success.

The Effect of God's Existence

The presence of God is a game-changer in every circumstance. When God is with you, obstacles become stepping stones, and enemies are rendered helpless. We invite God into our lives through our personal commitment and thirst for Him, which ensures that we are never overcome by life's obstacles.

Do not forget these:

Numbers 13:32–33 (TLB) remind us that our difficulties seem much worse when God is absent. Giants appear in place of midgets when there is no God, but even the highest mountains are reduced to stones when there is a God.

A daily practice of personal devotion to God is required. Our lives are given strength, clarity, and direction in this place of togetherness.

Unusual Elevation through Devotion

According to Psalm 37:23 (KJV), God directs the actions of the righteous. God's arrangement for our steps results in walking in His favor and living as a testament to His goodness.

Do Not Forget These:

Your destiny to greatness lies in personal devotion, obedience, and divine direction. Your extraordinary lifting reflects how deeply you have dedicated yourself to God.

Points of Action:

1. Make your commitment to God your priority. Allocate a specific period each day to seek Him, pay attention to His voice, and invite Him into every aspect of your life.

2. Continue to be spiritually ready. Victories in life are gained in the secret area of friendship with God.

3. Recognize the influence of teaching. Place yourself in settings where the anointing of God is being released, and be receptive to absorbing it.

4. Develop an appetite for God's presence. Allow your passion for God to surpass any obstacles or diversions you may encounter.

5. Create enduring bonds with outstanding individuals. Encircle yourself with people as dedicated to spiritual excellence and progress as you are.

CHAPTER 12

INSTRUCTIONS FOR UNUSUAL LIFTING: A CALL TO ELEVATE EVERY AREA OF LIFE (PART B)

During periods of exceptional lifting, everyone is expected to "step up their game." This calls for deliberate work in many spheres of our lives—spiritually and practically. This chapter describes five essential areas that anyone who wants to achieve their mission and experience divine uplift must improve.

1. Fellowship and personal devotion to life

First, our relationship and commitment to God need to be elevated. A close, profound relationship with the Creator is built on fellowship. It entails being in His presence, learning from Him, and letting Him interpret what happens in life. But fellowship and intercession are not the same thing. In devotion, we cultivate a relationship with God, while in mediation, the goal is to utilize prayer to reorganize spiritual processes.

Every believer should make intercession a regular practice in their lives. It entails persistent, focused prayer that disrupts and obstructs the enemy's schemes. In 2 Kings 6:8–11 (TLB), we witness Elisha's persistent disruption of the enemy's plans thanks to his heavenly insight. Interference is a proactive strategy since it thwarts the enemy's plans before implementation. Faithful, great men and women don't wait for fights to come to them before acting. Instead, they maintain their advantage by deflecting the enemy's darts via persistent prayer and intercession.

2. **Up Your Intercession Life**

Your life as an intercessor is one of the most important things to improve. Different from universal devotion, mediation fills the void and reorganizes spiritual environments. You can "intercept" enemy arrows before they land by acting as an intermediary. By interfering with the enemy's plans, we can avert possible catastrophes and lessen their power over us. Fewer arrows are deflected when we don't participate in mediation, making us more susceptible.

Our lives become more precarious the fewer arrows we can intercept. On the other hand, our destinies are more secure the more arrows we intercept through intercession. We sabotage and agitate the enemy's schemes by persistent prayer and obtaining divine assistance and favor. Intercession is the supernatural tool that enables us to protect our futures and interfere in the enemy's spiritual affairs.

3. **Up Your Adoration Life**

Increasing your devotional life is crucial, even beyond intercession. Adoration brings you into harmony with God's will and purpose. Through worship, we acknowledge God's sovereignty in our lives and show our love and respect for Him. The Bible is replete with examples of how worship changes environments and calls God's presence into them. True worship is a commitment that opens doors to uncommon lifting and the divine's resources, richness, and wisdom.

Adoration is a way of life that centers everything around God rather than just singing hymns. It necessitates humility, selflessness, and a strong desire to communicate with God. By making adoration our top priority, we set ourselves up to receive insights and divine direction beyond our human limitations.

4. Up Your Excellence Life

Another crucial aspect that needs to be prioritized is the quest for excellence. Proverbs 8:1-36 (MSG) highlights the significance of quality and intelligence in whatever we undertake. Being exceptional entails going above and beyond the ordinary and aiming for the best in all spheres of life, including our relationships, jobs, and ministries. Being exceptional draws exceptional people to you and sets you apart in any activity. We commit to diligence and continuous progress when we embrace excellence as our mindset.

The command to "go up to the mountain and bring wood" in Haggai 1:8 (KJV) is a metaphor for getting ready to construct something for God. This could entail obtaining the abilities, know-how, and materials required for the modern Christian to establish God's kingdom. For those who want to experience unique elevation, pursuing excellence—whether in evangelism, church expansion, or service to the body of Christ—is a must.

God asks us to bring "wood " to build His house. This implies that we have to invest consciously in spiritual and useful abilities that advance His kingdom. To be exceptional, one must be devoted to learning and constantly work to help others.

5. Up Your Wisdom Life

A valuable gem on the path to heavenly elevation is wisdom. Wisdom extends an invitation to a feast of comprehension, discernment, and life, according to Proverbs 9:1-6 (MSG). Wisdom helps us avoid pitfalls that could endanger our lives, make intelligent decisions, and deal with difficult situations. Our pursuit of knowledge leads to greater alignment with God's purpose and more tremendous success in all facets of life.

Seeking wisdom means making a conscious effort to read the Bible, spend time in prayer, and learn from others. It also entails surrounding yourself with sage advice and having the humility to accept guidance. Proverbs 8 warns against stupidity because it might end in devastation and catastrophe. We must actively seek intelligence because intelligence is the basis of all achievement.

The Influence of Spiritual Authority and Night Vigils

Night vigils are a highly effective activity to incorporate into your devotional and intercessory lives. Attending night vigils regularly —at least twice a week—significantly affects spiritual authority. Believers can obtain divine revelations, wage more intense spiritual warfare, and gain power over the enemy by praying at night.

Daniel gives an example of how fervent prayer might bring about heavenly intervention and topple established political authorities in Daniel 10:12–13 (TLB). His nocturnal watch and intercession brought angelic assistance and vanquished spiritual resistance. We unlock spiritual authority and power when we participate in night vigils; the same is true for us now.

Using discretion to protect spiritual matters

Another crucial lesson for extraordinary lifts is learning to guard spiritual concerns with prudence. Not every revelation or calling is meant to be shared with others. Personal spiritual matters need to be handled with caution. Sharing too much about your spiritual life exposes you to unwarranted attacks and spiritual warfare from others who might not be looking out for you.

Nahum 1:9 (KJV) states that affliction is born by evil imagination. As such, you must exercise wisdom to protect your prayer life and spiritual experiences. When people learn of your spiritual development, they can imagine negative things about you. If you don't cancel these projections, they may impede your spiritual growth and negatively impact your destiny.

Self-Restraint and Accountability

According to Proverbs 25:28 (KJV), a person without self-control is like a city with broken walls. To experience remarkable lifts, you must learn self-control in all facets of your life. This entails managing your feelings, ideas, and behavior. It also entails accepting accountability for your spiritual advancement.

Taking accountability entails giving up blaming other people or things for your lack of success. It involves accepting your calling, praying for wisdom from God, and taking initiative in your quest for achievement. By practicing self-control, you can set yourself up for higher levels of spiritual and personal development.

The Distribution of Knowledge, Resources, and Wealth

We set ourselves up for extraordinary raising as we elevate our friendship, intercession, adoration, excellence, and wisdom. According to Proverbs 8:32–36 (MSG), waiting on God is a wise way to spend one's life. When the timing is right, God bestows money, wisdom, and resources on those who follow Him faithfully.

It's crucial to understand that there will be difficulties along the way. Many people find themselves "filling with death" when they don't seek knowledge and follow God's plan for their lives. However, divine favor, promotion, and long-term success are guaranteed for those who follow these directions for unique lifting.

Thus, let us pledge to improve in all facets of our lives and grow into astute custodians of the callings and gifts that God has given us. We will walk in the authority God has appointed for us and experience the fullness of His lifting via dedication, intercession, excellence, and wisdom.

CHAPTER 13

QUALITIES OF GREAT PEOPLE

A yearning for greatness

T hose with an insatiable thirst for greatness are drawn to exceptional people. This hunger is not easily satisfied or extinguished. As Michael Jordan's coach doubted him because of his slim physique, Jordan's mother believed otherwise. She understood that greatness doesn't simply fall into anyone's lap; it is earned through relentless drive and effort. Nothing works until you're willing to work it.

Handling precious things

Magnificent people look for those who can handle valuables and treasures with diligence and care. According to Matthew 7:6 (TPT), those who are unable to handle valuable items sometimes condemn those who create them. As such, it is imperative that you surround yourself with people who understand the importance of living a life of sacrifice. Living carelessly can appear simple at first, but eventually, it gets difficult. Only those who live consciously preserve their treasures; careless ones never do.

The Power of Loyalty

Above all, great people value loyalty. Luke 9:23 (TPT) highlights how crucial it is to maintain loyalty in the face of difficulties.

Loyalty is essential to success. Solomon ascended to the throne due to his father David's loyalty. Similarly, Bathsheba's admiration for David's grandeur sprang from her understanding of his value rather than passion. People that support you when you most need strength are being loyal. Although talent wanes, devotion is bred by constancy.

Dealing with Toxicity

Toxic people steer clear of it at all costs. Certain people's impact on your life is so poisonous that not even ten detox procedures could get rid of them. Toxicity impedes and prevents growth. Great people will notice those who can live simply and gracefully in adversity. According to John 1:6 (KJV), there once was a man named John who God sent; similarly, those sent on divine missions must stay pure to accomplish their goals.

Surviving Pressure

Stress frequently makes our underlying poison visible. Greatness's demands reveal vulnerabilities, but the people who can withstand them and come out on top are the ones who succeed. Elisha's perseverance in the face of Elijah's testing is described in 2 Kings 2:6–9 (TLB). Ruth's commitment to Naomi in Ruth 1:16 (TLB) illustrates steadfastness in the face of difficulty.

Personal devotion and elevation

The secret to overcoming obstacles is selflessness—those who disregard the necessity of devotion risk depleting the reserves necessary for greatness. When devotion is lacking, life is viewed through lenses that warp reality. The Bible removes these filters, making one's destiny truthful without exaggerating or underestimating it. An open mind and heart, free from the poison of self-deception, are necessary for true greatness.

A non-toxic heart and genuine worship

A non-toxic heart is eager to learn and is receptive to God. Listening to heavenly guidance, particularly during prayer, is the source of greatness. According to Genesis 32:22–24 (TLB), God is your blesser rather than your wrestler. Giving up to God brings blessings; fighting Him brings trouble. Toxicity hardens the heart, making it impossible to embrace God's message.

Remember, greatness draws greatness. Great individuals always demand people with a toxic-free heart, hunger, loyalty, and endurance.

CHAPTER 14

THE FOUNDATIONS OF GROWTH AND WISDOM

A strong foundation is necessary for everything that endures, including relationships, careers, and spiritual development. Think of them as pillars. However, these foundations are frequently disregarded, particularly when people choose flimsy or fast repairs. Still, some things in life can't be completed with any amount of short-term work. While some tasks can be completed by the "maids" of wisdom, others call for wisdom in its most basic form.

The voice of wisdom tells us, "I am pure; use me." However, many people make the mistake of relying on the "maids" of wisdom —shortcuts that only provide momentary respite—instead of experiencing the richness that wisdom has to offer. We are in turmoil and an end-time spirit that feeds on chaos. It is wisdom that provides vision and direction amidst this uncertainty. However, you must make a conscious effort to understand this insight and feel this clarity. It doesn't happen by chance or just by hoping to know. Seeking the truth and being receptive to what it exposes demands purposeful effort and conscious decision.

1. Knowing with Intention

Intentionality is one of the cornerstones of a healthy relationship with God and oneself. It's not like you "know" by accident. You have to pursue your goals, whether related to spirituality, personal development, or even making sense of the experiences in your life. At a certain point in your life, you must come clean to God and ask Him to show you everything about yourself—your most outstanding qualities and flaws.

I once provided infertility therapy to a woman. After much prayer and thought, I had to break the news to her: she had married a man with numerous spiritual wives; therefore, her issue wasn't physical but somewhat spiritual. She broke off contact with me for six months because she was upset with me. Her spouse became pregnant by another lady while having an affair. Eventually, she called me again after he'd left her, taking everything with him. Would you believe that I warned you? I told her to let go, forgive him, and put her mind on God, even though she was inconsolable.

She was initially unable to follow through. Her obsession turned into stalking both the other woman and her husband. But her life changed drastically the moment she let go of him and focused on God. She became a prosperous and successful woman after being married again and naturally giving birth to twins. She and I learned a valuable lesson from this experience: although many people find it difficult to accept, the truth is also the road to freedom.

2 Truth and Growth's Power

For many Christians, telling them the truth—especially about themselves—is the worst thing you can do. Rejection has emerged as one of the biggest obstacles to progress in the modern world. In addition to bodily disorders, diseases that result in the rejection of truth—whether it originates from God or others—also claim the lives of a significant number of people.

We must be careful in our spiritual journeys and not take things for granted. You cannot rely on your past successes or believe they will help you win today's struggles. Development is an ongoing process. Like I say, "When will you mature? As you mature." Spiritual growth cannot be replaced and is not something that just happens. A feeble spirit is among the most hazardous things you can have around you. You cannot overcome obstacles or even realize your conflicts without a strong spirit.

To develop, you must accept your place in the world and launch "missiles" in all directions, engaging the enemy from every angle. This is a forceful, deliberate act with a strong foundation in wisdom—not a passive one. You must also insist on being aware of everything in your life. You have to come before God and confess your nakedness. Show me who you are. Show me not only my shortcomings but also my greatness." God will reveal both to you, not to condemn you but to assist you in becoming who He has called you to be.

3 The Importance of Patience and Divine Timing

Another virtue that many people ignore is patience, which wisdom also imparts. In the haste to succeed or to "get there," individuals frequently overlook God's schedule. The Holy Spirit is a guide who makes particular revelations at the appropriate times, but to enter that divine timing, we must be prepared to let go of our perplexity and fear. One saying that I like is "Leave to live." The confusion and dread we cling to thwart a meaningful existence frequently.

You create room for divine revelation when you let go of those doubts and anxieties. You realize that nothing in your life is pointless or random—everything has a purpose. God will make the path you intend to take evident. to walk—but only if you're prepared to let go of things that don't benefit you.

I had experienced a circumstance when I knew there would be an impartation, so I fasted after church. I was so overcome by the presence of God that I refrained from eating until after I had completed praying for the members. "It would be unfair for anyone to miss this impartation," I reminded myself. It takes a certain kind of commitment and endurance to wait for God's will. It requires faith that His timing is suitable and that one is willing to sit in His presence even when it is uncomfortable or inconvenient.

4 The Spiritual Life's Use of Passion

A further essential component is enthusiasm. You have to be careful not to let your love for God wane. It can be easy to allow the flame of your love for Him to fade as time goes on and difficulties appear. However, this enthusiasm maintains your connection to the almighty source of all knowledge and strength.

Imagine if every person in the crowd who claimed to have touched Jesus had done it intentionally. What if He had been moved by their desire to be more understanding, patient, or tuned in to heavenly treasure? The experience of the power would have been transformative for them. The same power is still available to us, but only if we approach God fervently and intentionally.

5 Divine Choosing and Your Special Place in It

Lastly, wisdom informs us that each person's life serves a purpose. Every person is called to play a specific job, and associated with that calling is a divine selection, a particular "wine" that fulfills your life's needs. Ephesians 5:18 reminds us to be filled with the Spirit rather than become inebriated with wine. This filling provides us with the strength and clarity to accomplish our goals.

In our day, God is training a few individuals to become spiritual generals. I know this because, in 1998, He told me that He was teaching 12 people worldwide to be among the strongest. This is about carrying out a divine duty, not glorying in one's own right.

You need these pillars—intentionality, truth, patience, passion, and wisdom—to rise to the occasion of your calling. God's "unusual rise and elevation" for your life can only come to pass at that point.

CHAPTER 15

LIVING AS HEAVEN'S REPRESENTATIVE

My spiritual father once told me this vital truth: "You must be Heaven's representative on earth." This idea captures the significance of our calling as Christians. God is not physically present because He is here. After all, we are His children. We must act in His name, reflecting His will and intent in all we do.

It's not an easy task. Being a spokesperson of Heaven entails having the responsibility to effect change in people's lives, relationships, and even in entire generations. It's simple to go through life without realizing how big of a responsibility this is, but everything changes when you do.

Taking Responsibility for Your Generation

Among the most depressing things we must ask ourselves is: What has my existence taught me? God won't inquire about your comfort level or the quantity of material goods you have when you meet Him. Instead, He will ask, "What has changed because of you since the day you were born?" This is about your influence on your family, church, and community, not just your achievements.

Has your family improved because of you? Have you made an impact on your church that honors God? Are you making a difference in the community where you live? You should base all of your actions and decisions on these inquiries. You must take care of the spiritual environment surrounding you as the representative of Heaven on Earth. It is the responsibility of your generation to effect change.

Heaven's Accountability

The truth of this obligation ought to challenge us rather than intimidate us. Imagine meeting with God after your time on earth has ended, and He asks you, "What did you do with the life I gave you?" Will you be able to respond with assurance? Will you be able to identify improvements brought about by your presence?

Although intimidating, this degree of accountability is also inspiring. It implies that you carry out a sacred duty and that your deeds count. Because of God's presence within you, something should change when you enter a room. When you interact with people, your love, generosity, and wisdom should make them feel like they are in heaven.

Turning into a Tool for God's Purpose

There are two types of people in this world: those who oppose God's work and those who flow with Him, opening themselves up to become channels for change. Some people dedicate their time to disparaging, discrediting, and assaulting others, attempting to change the world. They refuse to participate in the work of God's kingdom and instead concentrate on what is wrong. However, we are called to be the cause of why things improve in our families, neighborhoods, and churches as Heaven's delegates.

When you pass away, what will others say about you? Will people perceive you as someone who improved things and had a positive influence? Or will your departure be so insignificant that no one will miss you? This question pushes us to live intentionally and purposefully.

Making a Permanent Impression

Not dying is the ultimate tragedy; it leads a life without significance. When you serve as Heaven's envoy, you are expected to leave an impact transcending your time here on Earth. People should miss you not only for your personality but also for the divine influence you had.

Your life should be an example of God's grandeur so that when you are gone, there will be a discernible hole left behind. When you're gone, what will we miss? This question should motivate you to live each day with the goal of changing the world. Your life is designed to be light, guiding others toward God, whether in your neighborhood, church, or family.

Following God's Will

Living as a representation of Heaven requires you to live by God's plan. It means going with the flow, paying attention to where He leads, and actively engaging in His work. This call is not passive. You must engage with the surroundings and seek opportunities to make positive changes.

When you walk by God's will, you become a change agent. You start to perceive the world as He does, identifying the places that require reform, restoration, and healing. Things start to get better because of you. You are fulfilling your mission as God's spokesperson, which allows everyone around you to encounter God's love, grace, and truth.

An Appeal for Input

This chapter serves as a rallying cry. Remind yourself that your presence here is not by coincidence. Your life has a purpose, and you were put here on this planet for a reason. However, intentionality is needed to achieve that goal. You have to take responsibility for the changes that occur within your generation. "What is better because of me?" is a question you must ask yourself.

Don't let the opportunity to change things pass you by. Seek God's will for your life and walk in obedience to His calling to begin now. Be the reason your town is optimistic, your family is more robust, and your church is more active. Your life becomes a reflection of God's splendor when you live as an envoy of Heaven, which is a legacy you should leave behind.

CHAPTER 16

PROPHETIC DECLARATION AND PRAYERS

PRAYER 1:
Father, in the name of Jesus, by Your power and authority, by Your grace and mercy—we make demands on the impartation of this service. I receive the grace to catch everything that heaven has appropriated for me. In the mighty name of Jesus. (Luke 1:34-38 AMP)

PRAYER 2:

Father, in the name of Jesus, by Your power and authority, by Your grace and mercy—I receive the impartation that will unlock my life's value and meaning. As You up my game, I will enjoy supernatural, unusual rise and elevation. The hand that takes men up unusually will come upon me. The power that unusually lifts men and women will come upon me today. I celebrate good things and a good life. I reject a wrong life, meaningless. Today, my father and I are up my game because of this impartation. I receive Your grace to reveal Your glory. I stretch forth my hands towards Your altar and receive life, an armful of life. I receive clarity, direction, inspiration, and revelation. Whatever you have spread on the dining table for me, I receive. I leave my improvised confusion, and I live. I walk up the streets to a meaningful life with Your wisdom. In the mighty name of Jesus. (Proverbs 8:1-36 MSG; Proverbs 9:1-6 MSG; Proverbs 25:28 KJV; Proverbs 22:7 TPT)

PRAYER 3:

Father, in the name of Jesus, by Your power and authority, by Your grace and mercy—I receive a supernatural baptism of sanity, destiny sanity, mental, emotional, and life-long sanity. O Lord, I receive the wisdom that comes from above. I receive excellence, and as I live for You, I devote myself, connect with mediation, and reveal adoration. I live honoring You, and my entire life will produce excellence. I receive wisdom and reveal discretion. I walk up the street of a life with meaning. I declare what I couldn't achieve by my might or struggle the past 10 years, I will achieve in the next 1 year because of this impartation. I reject every evil arrow fired by those who thought my life was a threat to their lives. By Your power, wealth, and glory must accompany me, as well as substantial honor and a good name. No power can corrupt my name. I walk up the street of life with meaning in the mighty name of Jesus. (Proverbs 8:1-36 MSG; Proverbs 9:1-6 MSG; Proverbs 25:28 KJV; Proverbs 22:7 TPT; Psalms 112:5 KJV/TPT)

PART THREE

CHAPTER 17

THE POWER OF LOVE IN A RELATIONSHIP WITH GOD

The Vital Role of Love in the Advancement of God's Work

L ove is the thread that links God and man together in a complex way. Romans 8:28 (TPT) emphasizes a fundamental truth: those who love God allow Him to function in and through them. It is true that a person's love for God changes and fluctuates and that God's work in your life slows down when your love for God wanes. The foundation of God's unceasing involvement in our lives is our love for Him. Without love, this divine mission ends, leaving us immobile. As long as our hearts are burning brightly with love for Him, His hand will continue to shape and guide us. Our genuine love for God makes it possible to carry out his work in our lives. But God's work in our lives and the purpose He has for us are impermanent as soon as that love diminishes.

Love is the driving force behind God's goals, not just a sentiment. The more we love God, the more He can handle the details of our lives. This spiritual relationship comes from love. When we lose our love for God, it's as if we cut off communication with the one thing that gives us strength. Thus, we must nurture and cling to our love for God so that He can fulfill His purpose in our lives. Decreased love leads to missed opportunities, unfulfilled dreams, and spiritual stagnation.

The Consequences of a Reduced Love

Our commitment to God is not consistent. It fluctuates, and when it begins to decline, we feel the consequences in every area of our lives. The Bible tells of God's patience as He waits for our obedience to His will. However, God's work may stop if we don't patiently return the favor.

One example of what happens when someone refuses to give God total authority over every aspect of their life is the story of Hagar in Genesis 16:6–9 (TLB). Hagar chose to run away from Sarah rather than surrender because of her arrogance. God requested that Hagar, who was in charge of deciding her fate, surrender to her instead of Abraham. Similarly, when we refuse to allow God to use certain facets of our lives in His more excellent plan, we delay God's purpose. Our stubborn determination to cling to some parts of our lives results in unresolved sadness, unfinished stories, and unfulfilled potential.

The enslaved people fled as soon as there was an issue. Like Hagar, many Christians run from problems as soon as they emerge or meet difficulties in their connection with God, not understanding that these trials are vital to the masterpiece He is constructing in their life. All challenges, all misfortunes, and even the results of bad choices are strands woven together by the divine. However, when we break those threads by murdering someone, we leave holes and flaws in the story that God is trying to tell through our lives.

God's Design and the Importance of Waiting

Patience is a crucial element that enhances love in our relationship with God. Romans 8:28 (TPT) tells us that nothing in our lives is wasted when we love God. No matter how challenging or inconsequential something may seem, God utilizes it all for a purpose greater than ourselves. But patience is required to see how these parts are combined to make something magnificent.

God sees everything that happens in our lives. Everything has a purpose in the grand scheme of things, even the hardships, obstacles, and suffering. However, many Christians are not patient enough to wait for God's perfect timing. They look for quick fixes for their problems and practical solutions for their suffering. But God's ways are well-thought-out, and His work is laborious. He cannot reveal His plans for our lives if we go too fast or give up too soon.

An excellent example is Saul, who discovered his destiny in 1 Samuel 9:5–19 (TLB) rather than his father's donkeys. Saul had no idea God had prepared him for his throne using the missing donkeys. If Saul had given up looking for the donkeys and returned home immediately, he may never have encountered the prophet Samuel and ultimately received his heavenly appointment as king. In contrast, trivial or bothersome situations could occur in our lives, yet they often act as a conduit via which God leads us to our destiny. A piece of art appears disorganized and incomplete when examined in parts, and our lives can also appear fractured when viewed through a limited lens. But since God sees the overall picture, He is patient as He arranges the pieces to form a meaningful and logical whole. If we lack patience, we might give up before the puzzle is finished, leaving us with a pointless, disjointed life.

The Consequences of Insufficient Patience

Anger can be detrimental to our relationship with God. We may give up before we see the results, believing that certain aspects of our lives are meaningless or insignificant. But as Paul says in Romans 8:28 (TPT), "God works all things together for good." This includes the things we cannot understand, the difficult moments, and even the mistakes we commit. For example, John

D. Rockefeller could have easily dismissed his complicated family history as irrelevant or detrimental to his future. But God used the same circumstances to make him one of the wealthiest people of his time, and his legacy has continued for many years. Like Rockefeller, we may not understand why we are having trouble, but if we wait patiently, God will reveal how even our challenges have a greater meaning.

CHAPTER 18

THE PUZZLE OF
LIFE AND GOD'S
INTENTIONS

L ife often feels like a cluttered, complex puzzle with random pieces that don't seem to fit together or are even contradictory. Nevertheless, all the parts of our lives, joyous or sad, have a specific position and function in the greater plan of God's design. This chapter delves into the nature of life's puzzles and the all-powerful ability of God to bring the various facets of our existence together into a cohesive whole.

Solving the Mysteries of Life

Life's puzzles often stem from confusion, misfortune, and unrelated gifts. When we encounter challenges or situations we do not fully comprehend; it is easy to feel as though we are staring at a pile of puzzle pieces and have no idea how they will fit together.

Romans 8:28 (TPT), which gives us a clear understanding of how God works in our lives, says that we are his lovers called to fulfill his designed purpose. For this reason, we are convinced that every aspect of our lives is constantly woven together to fit into God's perfect plan of bringing good into our lives. In this chapter, the apostle Paul tells Christians that God is continuously at work and uses every detail—good or bad—to further His more extensive plan.

Our lives are not disconnected or pointless. However, it is often not immediately apparent to us how they cooperate. It's common to feel like our lives are in disorder when there's a storm or uncertainty. But God, the All-Powerful Weaver, has a grand scheme, and He uses all of our experiences to reveal His ultimate plan.

Genesis 16's account of Hagar illustrates how challenging life's issues may be. As a pregnant runaway slave, Hagar's life must have appeared to be a confusing and chaotic maze. After taking advantage of her, Sarah and Abraham abandoned her. God had a plan even though it was a difficult time for her. The Lord's angel found Hagar and told her to return, promising that her son Ishmael would become a mighty nation. What seemed like a mistake or a dead end was part of God's larger plan for her life.

In a similar spirit, everything that occurs in our lives—even the seemingly insignificant things, missed opportunities, or difficult periods—is part of God's larger plan. In God's hands, nothing is wasted, and everything matters.

How God Puts All the Pieces of Our Lives Together

God is constantly at work piecing our lives together. The phrase "weaving" inspires visions of painstaking, meticulous work resulting in a harmonious and gorgeous design. Like a weaver who weaves numerous colors of yarn into an elaborate design, God takes the various, and often unpleasant, portions of our existence and incorporates them into His marvelous creation.

When weaving, it's important to remember that not every thread is glossy and smooth. Some are twisted, coarse, or dark. These represent the challenges, setbacks, and heartaches we experience. But God utilizes the blessings and problems in our lives to form us into the people He has called us to be, just as a great weaver employs bright and dark threads to create contrast and depth.

Take a look at Saul's story in 1 Samuel 9. After all, Saul discovers he is supposed to be the king of Israel while looking for his father's lost donkeys. Saul did not realize at the time that God was using Saul's life specifics for a purpose beyond his current assignment. In addition to being a problem, his lost donkeys guided him in the direction of the prophet Samuel and, eventually, to his coronation. This narrative demonstrates how God might direct us toward a greater good, even in our existence's tedious or annoying facets.

One essential element is the idea that God is constantly weaving. In our lives, God is always at work. Perhaps we will eventually understand His plan when the parts fall into place. It may take some time for the entire picture to become apparent. This is why it takes patience and confidence to trust God to finish the work He has started in us.

One of the biggest challenges facing Christians is letting go of the parts of life that seem to be the most flawed. God wants to use these specific details to highlight His power and grace. However, if we cling to our pain or refuse to give God authority over some aspects of our lives, we risk missing out on the beauty God may create from our mess. God calls us to provide him with our problems so He can utilize them to make something beautiful, even if we may be tempted to run away from Him as Hagar did.

The Importance of Letting God Complete His Work

Without God's finished work, our lives are as incomplete as a puzzle when all the pieces are not in their proper places. In this case, patience is essential because it gives God the room and time to work in ways that are not immediately clear to us. We have to resist the need to force the pieces into position before God is ready to reveal to us how they fit together.

When we rush God or attempt to fix situations ourselves, we frequently make things worse for ourselves. Romans 8:28 reassures us that everything happens for the good of people who love God, including trials, blessings, and uncertainty. This does not mean we will avoid hardship; instead, it means that every aspect of our life functions in God's plan. We are responsible for trusting and waiting for Him to finish the image.

Another lesson from Hagar's narrative is the value of giving up. She longed to escape her situation, but God instructed her to return and submit to Sarah. Because of her obedience, God could continue working in her life. Similarly, we must give God authority over our existence's broken and fragmented parts. Through this submission, God may complete His work in us.

Though the details of our journey may seem overwhelming at times, God is never surprised by them. He understands every phase from beginning to end and how they all work together. Even the parts that seem to be mistakes or breakdowns are essential to the plan. The lessons we learn, and the pain we endure are part of the process that shapes us into the image of Christ. As our faith grows, we begin to see the beauty of God's creation in our daily lives. A life that glorifies God comprises all seemingly unrelated events, highs and lows, and even the waiting and perplexing seasons. Our lives are a living example of God's power, grace, and love.

CHAPTER 19

SUBMISSION AND TRANSFORMATION: LESSONS FROM HAGAR

T he story of Hagar shows us how submitting to God's will can have unfathomable consequences for our lives. It is deep and complex at the same time. Hagar, an enslaved Egyptian, is drawn into a complex web of human decisions, emotions, and divine plans. Her story teaches us to be humble, to own up to our faults, and to trust in God's mighty plan of redemption. Analyzing her journey, we uncover what it means to surrender our lives to God's direction and how that surrender brings about change.

Hagar's Embarrassment and Deference

The Bible presents Hagar as Sarai's discontent with God's promise to deliver Abraham as a son. In Genesis 16, Sarai proposes to Abraham Hagar to conceive a child through her. This arrangement brings about discord. Hagar reacts to her pregnancy more arrogantly than modestly. Genesis 16:4 states, "She began to despise her mistress when she knew she was pregnant."

Hagar was proud to have been given the role of mother

to Abraham's kid. Most likely feeling better than Sarai, who remained infertile. But all she accomplished was inflame family tensions with her haughty manner. Because Hagar felt Sarai's treatment of her had degraded her, she ran into the wilderness. Perhaps Hagar's actions were just a natural conceit in response to her circumstances—given that she was carrying Abraham's successor—but her attitude was a consequence of her mistaken perception of her place in God's purpose.

Arrogance often creeps in when we lose sight of the bigger vision and focus primarily on the temporary requirements of success or advancement. Hagar considered her pregnancy a personal honor rather than a mandate from God, even though it was a part of God's more excellent plan. Her hubris prevented her from seeing the bigger picture God had in store for her and her son, Isaac. In an identical spirit, we occasionally allow our advantages or successes to exaggerate our importance, forgetting that everything we possess is a gift from God and serves His purpose. A proud attitude can lead to disobedience, which pushes us away from the people and places God has called us to grow and learn.

However, God intervenes kindly. When Hagar flees into the wilderness, her story does not end. When she runs into the Lord's angel, he instructs her to return to Sarai and obey her. The words of the angel are found in Genesis 16:9: "Go back to your mistress and submit to her." Hagar goes through a significant turning point at this time when she realizes that surrendering is a means of atonement and transformation rather than just a passive act of obedience.

Admitting Our Mistakes

Hagar's story demonstrates that our flaws and mistakes need not define who we are. Her escape and arrogance were errors, yet they opened the door to a deeper connection with God. The Bible does not hide the human side of its characters; Hagar is one of us; she reacts rashly to difficult situations, just like many of us do.

But Hagar is receiving healing from God instead of punishment for her sins. The angel of the Lord does not punish her; instead, he guides her and assures her that her son will be rewarded. "I will increase your descendants so much that they will be too numerous to count," declares Genesis 16:10. *God's promise is still valid despite her initial mistakes.* He does not alter His intentions in response to her mistakes; instead, He leverages them to accomplish His sacred purpose.

This portion of Hagar's journey teaches us an important lesson: God uses our mistakes to develop us. If we allow it, those moments may even make us more aware of God's purpose, even though we may regret certain decisions or deeds later. God's responsibility is to turn our errors into chances for growth and development. When we make mistakes before God, they become opportunities for growth, self-humbling, and understanding the scope of God's grace.

Hagar made the error of hating Sarai and fleeing into the wilderness because she could not understand the importance of submission. She perceived her circumstances through the lenses of competitiveness and vanity rather than as part of God's larger plan. We are also vulnerable to this temptation when we allow pride, fear, or annoyance to drag us away from our proper position in God's plan and toward our immediate circumstances.

Hagar's willingness to grow from her error makes her story so unique. Following the angel's guidance, she returns to where she intends to flee. **Her obedience makes it possible for God to bless her and Isaac.** Similarly, when we submit and humble ourselves before God's plan, we make room for His redeeming work in our lives.

Redemption by Submission to God

Submission is one of the most potent elements in Hagar's narrative. Even though giving in to authority might be challenging, Hagar finds redemption in this act of surrender, especially after being wronged. God did not give Hagar orders to persecute others; instead, He encouraged her to trust in His omnipotence. Hagar returned to Sarai and offered herself up to God, trusting that He would sustain her and honor His promise.

Believing that God is in control, even when we don't fully understand His plan, is the cornerstone of the Christian life. The essence of surrender is this: When we submit to God and His authority, we accept His wisdom and let go of our need to control every part of our lives. He now rules over us. Putting your faith in God and following His direction is a conscious choice, even when it seems unclear or uncomfortable. To submit is not to be indifferent.

Hagar returned to Sarai, demonstrating her trust. She had no guarantee that Sarai would treat her better or that things would immediately improve. But God could work in her life because she followed. Genesis 21 recalls the fulfillment of God's promise to Hagar when a sizable nation takes in Ishmael. Hagar's submission guaranteed both her survival and the well-being of her progeny.

The story of God's deliverance via Hagar's submission is not unique to her. This is a reality that all Christians should adhere to. We make ourselves susceptible to God's transformative power when we submit to Him. Romans 12:1-2 (NIV) tells us to present our bodies as a living sacrifice and to allow our thoughts to be renewed. One essential element of this shift is surrender. We become the people He has called us to be when we surrender to His plan, strengthening our faith and using us to accomplish His goals.

The story of Hagar serves as more evidence that God cares for and is conscious of the poor and marginalized. After the angel appears, Hagar addresses God as El Roi, meaning "the God who sees me. When she was at her lowest, feeling alone and abandoned, God gave her compassion and a promise. This is the central idea of redemption: God loves us despite our flaws and rewards us for doing what is right.

CHAPTER 20

THE PROPHETIC PROCESS IN DISCOVERING DESTINY

Finding one's destiny is a life-changing experience frequently accompanied by angelic visions and paranormal advice. The prophetic, or the capacity to discern God's purposes and designs for our lives and the world around us, is central to this process. Destiny is shaped and revealed through prophetic utterances, meetings with the divine, and prophetic encounters. Understanding these facets of the prophetic process might help us better understand how God guides us toward achieving His goals for our lives. This chapter will cover the significance of divine experiences, the role prophets play in determining our destiny, and how prophetic words can change our lives and help us fulfill our heavenly calling.

The Importance of Prophets in Shaping History

The Bible has a long and distinguished history of using prophets to speak for God and provide His people with direction, correction, and teaching. They have a profound effect on the fates of individuals and countries. From Moses to Elijah, Samuel to

John the Baptist, prophets have revealed God's will and changed people's individual and collective destiny. Regarding one's destiny, prophets act as God's delegates, providing direction, affirmation, and elucidation of God's will.

A clear biblical illustration is Samuel's anointing of David. Samuel gave a prophecy that marked the start of David's ascent to the Israeli monarchy (1 Samuel 16). Samuel's prophetic insight revealed God's plan for David, even though he was still a tiny shepherd lad. Even though it took years for this prophecy to come to pass, this was the turning point in David's rise from obscurity to monarchy. The prophetic word formed David's character and prepared him for the trials and triumphs ahead. David could never have reached his potential without Samuel's role in this process.

Prophets play more than just messengers when it comes to influencing destiny. Prophets frequently serve as transformative catalysts by clearly and powerfully communicating God's Word. They assist people in coordinating their lives with the divine plan by prophesying future events and providing real-time revelation of God's intent. Since many people must completely change their beliefs, actions, and choices to achieve this harmony, the prophetic process frequently seems exciting and challenging. People are led to a more profound comprehension of their identity and role in God's kingdom by the direction of prophetic voices.

Prophetic roles are still critical in today's world. Prophets inspire us to rise into the fullness of our destiny, even though we might not always understand the significance of what they have to say right away. They encourage trust and a burning desire to follow God's plan. Prophets are spiritual guides who enable us to follow the path God has planned for us. They also frequently validate the feelings God has already aroused within us.

The Importance of Spiritual Experiences

Divine encounters are transformative experiences in which God's power, love, and purposes for our lives are made evident to us. These interactions frequently represent turning points in realizing one's destiny. Scripture is replete with examples of how God works via supernatural encounters to change people's lives and reveal their unique calling.

One famous instance is the meeting of God and Moses in the burning bush (Exodus 3). At the time, Moses was a wandering shepherd who lived far from Egypt's splendor. However, God intended for Moses to serve as Israel's deliverer through this encounter. Not only was the burning bush a miraculous occurrence, but it was also a moment of destiny revelation when Moses was given the prophecy to lead his people out of slavery. After this experience, Moses changed from a man fleeing his past to a prophet and a nation's leader.

Divine experiences frequently occur during times of crisis or uncertainty, when people are disoriented, unsure of themselves, or feel cut off from their mission. God steps in during these times, giving direction and clarity. Another striking illustration is Jacob wrestling with the angel at Peniel (Genesis 32:22-32). Although duplicity and manipulation characterized Jacob's life, he struggled with identity and destiny throughout this supernatural encounter. At this point, God gave him the name Israel, which means "he who strives with God," instead of Jacob, which meant "supplanter." This meeting not only changed Jacob's destiny, but it also gave rise to a country.

The direct revelation of God's will is why divine encounters are significant. These encounters frequently validate past prophecies or unveil new facets of God's design for our lives. Some examples of divine encounters are dreams, visions, angelic visits, or a strong sense of God's presence during prayer. Not only is the supernatural component significant, but so is the message God conveys to us via these experiences—one that challenges us to greater degrees of obedience, change, and purpose alignment.

In the process of discovering destiny, heavenly encounters function as both landmarks and turning points. They help us recognize God's presence in our lives and move forward with a fresh sense of trust and resolve to follow our heavenly calling. These instances remind us that God is actively working through and in us to accomplish His purpose; we are not traveling this path alone.

How Prophecy Inspires Change

Words that predict the future can significantly change someone's life. Prophecy is one way that God speaks, not only to educate but also to transform. Prophecy weighs heaven, so embracing it with trust can bring about significant change.

Prophetic statements often provide clarity in situations that seem ambiguous or confusing. They illuminate the way ahead by acting as a beacon of light. But our activity is necessary for the transformation that comes after prophetic words. Faith, obedience, and endurance are required in response to God's communication through a prophet. Trials, tribulations, and personal development are frequently encountered on the path between hearing a prophetic word and witnessing its fulfillment.

The life of Joseph is a striking example of prophetic change. When Joseph was a young man, he was given dreams that predicted his future supremacy and authority (Genesis 37). However, numerous barriers stood in the way of achieving these goals. Before Joseph could become the leader of Egypt, he had to go through imprisonment, service, and betrayal. Not just because of the dreams he experienced but also because of his ongoing dedication to God throughout the process, which led to his conversion. He allowed the prophecy to shape his character, bolster his faith, and prepare him for his destined role.

Prophetic words push us to look beyond the present and match our actions with God's plan for the future. They can arouse spiritual gifts, strengthen faith, and elevate us to new heights of purpose. But prophetic words frequently require endurance and patience to come to pass. The gap between hearing a prophetic message and seeing its manifestation might be a testing and preparation period. God frequently works on our hearts during this season, preparing us to handle His destiny.

Prophetic utterances are instruments for transformation rather than just future forecasts. When a prophetic word comes to us, it must be nourished by prayer, faith, and action. We must believe that God will bring the message to pass in His perfect timing and enable it to alter our lives. Our destiny starts to pass as we surrender to the prophetic process.

CHAPTER 21

PROPHETIC UTTERANCES, PRAYERS FOR PROPHETIC ENCOUNTERS .

P rophetic Word of Knowledge:
"The Lord says there is someone here; you carry every load on your life with no help. After today, I will begin to send helpers before you. You will no longer carry it alone."

"The Lord said there is someone in this house; you have been writing exams but have not been passing the exam."

"The Lord said He wants to heal someone. The person has a medical issue, but that issue is over."

"Every medical issue or result that is giving you sleepless nights, by the power on this altar, is broken now in the name of Jesus."

"Somebody is experiencing the healing of God right now in the name of Jesus."

Prophetic Utterance of Divine Lifting:

"If you are crawling, this is your time to fast forward. If you are running, this is your time to fly. The sky is not our goal. Heaven is our base."

"When God lifts, He lifts beyond a level no man can explain."

"There is no level you are now that God can't change. God will put you above those you see ahead of you."

"When God is ready with you, your beauty will be different."

"When God is ready to lift a man, He makes you meet a man that has been lifted, and you discover that God will use that man for you."

"God doesn't come down to help anyone; He sends someone before you that can change your story."

Prophetic Declaration for Lifting and Promotion:

"You will no longer operate from below."

"When it's time to be lifted, your angels will not rest until you are lifted."

"It is your time for greatness and grace to come upon you."

Prophetic Word about Family Battles:

"Many of you were not born like this. It was a family war that made you like this. This is not the plan of God for you. It was a family battle that turned you to this level. This is not how God planned your life."

Prophetic Word/Prayer for Restoration:

"The Lord said He is about to restore His church. I hear restoration. God is bringing the lost sheep back. This will happen very quickly. I see the angel of evangelism going from house to house, waking the sleeping and redirecting them to Church on Fire International. God is bringing them."

Prophetic Insight and Promise for the Future:

"Before the 2nd half of the year is open, you will close the first half of this year singing good songs, new songs, the songs of lifting and celebration."

"We are entering into one of the most significant months of the decade, not just the year."

"What will happen tomorrow is that you will enter a place in the realm of the spirit that a signal people fast for 40 years to catch will be caught by you."

Prophetic Declaration for Healing:

"The Lord said there is someone with a pain that travels around your body; receive healing now."

Prophetic Declaration for Divine Help and Favor:

"Esther found favor. She was loved. She was preferred among others. That's what brings lifting—being preferred."

"Faithful is He that calls you and will do it."

"Joseph was lifted from prisoner to prime minister. He ruled in a strange land."

Prophetic Assurance of Victory:

"When God is ready to help you, your disability cannot stop you."

"It doesn't matter what they have been saying; now the saying is different!"

"My head will be lifted above those who said there is no help for me in God."

"You have to prove them wrong. The year we are in is such a strategic year."

Other Prophetic utterances

"This second half will celebrate your test and testimonies."

"The instruction needed to deliver you from destruction impending will be delivered to you."

"Instruction that will enable you to enter a new level of destiny construction."

"This is a prophetic shift. It means even that which you don't know belongs to you will come to you."

"Something has shifted in the spirit realm and is in your favor."

"I see grace for royalty and distinction."

"As you leave this place, you will have encounters."

"The very instruction you need will be downloaded to you."

"I see men and women walking in a glory they never thought they would walk in."

Prayer points

1. Father, in the name of Jesus, by Your power and authority, by Your grace and mercy, I believe You for unusual encounters this weekend. My life to command unusual results because of this prophetic encounter. Let there be a remarkable shift in my life, family, and destiny, resulting in my lifting and rise. Cause the heavens to respond to my rise and my earth to cooperate with my heavens in the mighty name of Jesus.

2. Father, in the name of Jesus, by Your power and authority, grace and mercy, I submit to You, my Helper. I cry out and ask that You intervene this night. By Your mercies, release prophetic grace and oil to turn my mockery into glory and my puzzle into words, sentences, and volumes. Give me encounters this weekend that will cause me to count on my generation. As I cross into the last month of this first half of the year, let my glory stream Your glory in the mighty name of Jesus.

3. Father, in the name of Jesus, by Your power and authority, by Your grace and mercy, take every fragment in my life and family and weave them into Your purpose so that my story will stream Your glory. Make every fragment make sense, and let the world feel the impact of my life in the mighty name of Jesus.

4. Father, in the name of Jesus, by Your power and authority, by Your grace and mercy, with Your powerful hand, lift me in the mighty name of Jesus.

5. Father, in the name of Jesus, by Your power and authority, by Your grace and mercy, I receive a promotion that every eye will see in the mighty name of Jesus.

6. Father, in the name of Jesus, by Your power and authority, by Your grace and mercy, from today, I will no longer operate from below; I will operate in a higher realm in the mighty name of Jesus.

7. Father, in the name of Jesus, by Your power and authority, by Your grace and mercy, every power working against my lifting, lose your grip over me in the mighty name of Jesus.

8. Father, in the name of Jesus, by Your power and authority, by Your grace and mercy, lift me beyond expectation. Lord, cause me to exceed every expectation in the mighty name of Jesus.

9. Father, in the name of Jesus, by Your power and authority, by Your grace and mercy, lift my head. Connect me with heaven's frequencies so that I will know what to do, not just to rise, but to stay up. Help me position for a favor, to come, stay, and grow. Let me know what to know and make the right moves so my head will be lifted above affliction, shame, and reproach in the mighty name of Jesus.

10. Father, in the name of Jesus, by Your power and authority, by Your grace and mercy, I declare every power assigned to keep me down is paralyzed. I receive whatever it takes to lift me as I enter the last month of this first half of the year. Every contradiction, complication, and contamination stays in May. You don't belong in June and can't cross over with me. Everything ugly, bitter, and wrong, you are turned into beauty in the mighty name of Jesus.

CONCLUSION

A Journey Into Spiritual Expansion And Elevation

A s we draw to a close on this life-transforming journey, we must consider the deep facts and spiritual discoveries we have studied throughout the chapters. This book is a real example of the strength of spiritual alignment, divine purpose, and pursuing a fantastic life in Christ rather than just a compilation of beneficial writings. From "Recognizing the Significance of Your Existence" to "The Prophetic Process in Discovering Destiny," every chapter has provided a stepping stone toward a greater comprehension of spirituality.

The overarching theme that has permeated these pages is unmistakable. Each person is unique, with a purpose, potential, and significance intimately interwoven into God's magnificent design.

This is an essential insight.

The moment you realize how important this is, everything else flows. You could float aimlessly without it, but with it, you can project yourself into your destiny and divine calling.

Why is the realization of who you are very Important?

It all started with an invitation to acknowledge the importance of your existence. Life becomes purposeful, a heavenly work of art rather than a collection of coincidental incidents.

Knowing this alters everything. Your perspective will change from survival to purpose when you realize you are a part of God's larger story. As discussed in Chapter 1, 'Recognizing the Significance of Your Existence,' knowing this gives you all the confidence you need.

Knowing your significance in God's larger scheme gives you the confidence to proceed.

This insight then drives you to Chapter 2, Project into Purpose. So, purpose is a continual exploration process instead of being a destination. You must realize this, and as you do, you can match your goals with God's plan and permit Him to guide you toward completing your heavenly mission.

Spiritual Alignment: A Key to Unlocking God's Blessings

The strength of spiritual alignment emerged as a significant theme throughout several chapters. Chapter 3 explored how God's benefits are accessible to those who agree with His will.

As we have seen through this journey, alignment comes up repeatedly because it is essential to unlocking God's purpose for your life. Even though you might put in a lot of effort and suffer in the absence of alignment, your efforts will be rewarded when you do because you will be able to work in perfect divine timing and receive an abundance of His grace.

Chapter 4 also examined what becoming a hub for God's blessings means. When we discussed being a hub for God's blessings, we turned our attention from getting to giving. When you align with God's purpose, you are blessed and given the ability to bless others.

This is how you become a channel for His blessings, turning from a mere recipient to an active participant in God's plan for His Kingdom.

Moving Up to Higher Responsibility Levels

Obstacles stand in the way of achieving purpose. Chapter 5 discusses the call to progress from "appetizers to the main course," which necessitates obedience and sacrifice. Chapter 7 underlines the significance of these two attributes for entering the Greater Realms of Responsibility.

Understanding the core ingredients of obedience and sacrifice is the key to unlocking the next phase of your calling. If you are to completely accept the divine purpose for your life, you must be prepared to let go of what is familiar and have faith in God's plan, even when it necessitates making tough decisions.

A key point in this path is realizing your divine calling, as we covered in Chapter 6. You can act with bravery and determination when you acknowledge the importance of your duty and recognize that God has prepared you for every task He has given you. Chapter 8 discussed how taking on more responsibility is a logical next step in your spiritual development. God never wants you to remain still; instead, He calls you to grow, thrive, and extend your impact across the Kingdom.

The Significance of Prophecy, Prayer, and Timing

Comprehending God's time and design is another essential trip component, as discussed in Chapter 9. Timing is crucial in God's Kingdom. Racing ahead or falling behind God's timing might result in missed chances or needless delays.

Doors open quickly, and when you are in sync with God's schedule, you find yourself in the right location at the right moment.

As Chapters 10 and 21 cover, the importance of prayer and prophetic utterances cannot be overestimated.

Prophetic utterances are divine statements that bring forth things that are not as though they were and speak life into your goal. Prayer is your lifeline to heaven and your direct path to the

Almighty God who controls your fate.

Only through prayer can you obtain supernatural insight, understanding, and direction, all of which are essential for overcoming the challenges of everyday life.

Chapters 11 and 12 presented the principle of instructions for unusual lifting and encouraged us to follow God's instructions to improve every aspect of life.

We must obey God's specific instructions to experience miraculous advancement and elevation, just as historical individuals such as Joseph, Esther, and David did.

Everyone who aligns with God's purpose and is willing to follow His lead is eligible for the promise of extraordinary elevation, not just a few chosen.

Living as the Symbol of Heaven

In Chapters 13 and 15, we examined the characteristics of exceptional individuals and the meaning of living as the emissary of heaven.

Greatness in God's Kingdom is not defined by accomplishment according to external standards but rather by a life lived in love, service, and humility. People who are empathic about kingdom and purpose understand that their lives reflect heaven, a living embodiment of God's character, values, and love in everything they undertake.

In Chapter 14, we examined the foundations of growth and wisdom. This serves as a reminder that intentionality is necessary for spiritual progress. The main thing is wisdom, which you must acquire to navigate life's challenges and accomplish your divine purpose.

The Transformational Power of Love and Submission

In Part Three of this journey, we entered the core of relationships: our connections with God and others. Chapter 17 discussed the power of Love in a Relationship with God, emphasizing that love is the cornerstone around which everything else is constructed.

Spiritual transformation and progress originate from a close, personal relationship with God.

In Chapter 18, we discussed God's intentions and the puzzle of life. Life frequently seems like a puzzle, but when we put our faith in God's purposes, we understand how every element fits into the larger picture to produce a great and mighty, stunning work of art.

In Chapter 19, we explored Hagar's story. She served as an example of transformation and the submissive power of obedience. Hagar's path shows us that surrendering to God's will can result in significant shifts and meaning, even in trying situations.

Accepting Prophecy-Based Destiny

Lastly, in Chapter 20 of Discovering Destiny, we focused on the prophetic process. Experiences and words of prophecy can make clear God's unique intentions for our lives. When we embrace the prophetic, we put ourselves in a position to receive heavenly guidance and insights that lead us to the accomplishment of our destiny.

Boldly Pursuing Your Divine Destiny

This journey has been one of self-discovery, spiritual harmony, and divine elevation. The lessons and revelations presented are not intended to be merely knowledge but transformative instruments that enable you to pursue your divinely appointed calling confidently.

This is when you have been called and have a special place in the larger scheme of God's Kingdom.

Remember that God has perfect timing, purpose, and plans for your life as you move forward. Continue to align yourself with His will, be steadfast in prayer, and accept the power of prophetic statements. It is up to you to seize the promise of extraordinary lifting and heavenly ascension.

I pray that you will miss these insights. Much more, may you walk fearlessly into the fullness of your calling, knowing that you play a big part in God's unique plan. I pray that today will start a life filled with strength, direction, and divine favor for you in Jesus' name. (Amen)

A SPECIAL CALL TO SALVATION & NEW BEGINNINGS FROM APOSTLE DR. DAVID PHILEMON

Dear Beloved,

God loves you deeply and has brought you to this moment for a reason. No matter your past, His love and forgiveness are available to you.

The Bible says in John 3:16, "For God so loved the world that He gave His one and only Son, that whoever believes in Him shall not perish but have eternal life." Jesus Christ came to save you, offering you a new life of purpose and peace.

If you're ready to accept Jesus as your Lord and Savior, pray this simple prayer:

The Salvation Prayer

"Heavenly Father, I come to You in the Name of Jesus. I acknowledge that I am a sinner in need of a Savior. I believe that

Jesus Christ is Your Son, that He died for my sins, and that You raised Him from the dead. I repent of my sins and turn to You with my

Whole heart. Jesus, I ask You to come into my life. Be my Lord and my Savior. I surrender my life to You. Fill me with Your Holy Spirit, guide me on the path of righteousness, and help me to follow Your script for my life. Thank you, Father, for saving me. In the name of Jesus. Amen."

Welcome to the Family of God!

If you have just prayed this prayer, Congratulations! You are now a child of God, and heaven is rejoicing. Your journey has begun, and we're here to support you as you grow in faith and discover God's unique plans for you.

Next Steps:

• Connect with a Bible-believing church.

• Read the Bible Daily: God's Word is your guide.

• Pray Regularly: Prayer is your lifeline to God.

• Share Your Faith: Don't keep the good news to yourself.

www.ingramcontent.com/pod-product-compliance
Lightning Source LLC
Chambersburg PA
CBHW060443040426
42331CB00044B/2570